200

FENG SHUI

FENG SHUI

ENVIRONMENTS OF POWER
A STUDY OF CHINESE ARCHITECTURE

Dr Evelyn Lip

*Dedicated to my filial son, Kenny Lip Yau Sueng and
my loving daughter, Jacqueline Lip Tzun Cheang.*

A.D. ACADEMY EDITIONS

Acknowledgements

First and foremost, I wish to express my sincere thanks to Associate Professor, Khoo Cheng Lim, the Dean of the Faculty of Architecture and Building, for his encouragement during the course of writing this book. The history of Chinese architecture has been one of the subjects I have been teaching at the School of Architecture, National University of Singapore, for the last twenty-six years of my academic life. I could not have written this book without his moral support.

This book would not be complete without the illustrative photographs of the Forbidden City, the Gugong, the Yi Heyuan, the Bishu Shanzhuang and some of the monuments and landscaped gardens taken by my son, Kenny Lip Yau Sueng. These beautiful photographs vividly present the magnificence and majesty of the buildings once used by the most powerful rulers of China. A special word of appreciation to Kenny not just for his works of art but also for his unceasing support during the course of visiting the sites, researching and writing this book.

My daughter, Jacqueline, has also given me unceasing moral support and continual encouragement during the preparation of this work. She deserves very special praise and appreciation.

I also wish to express my gratitude to the following people for their moral support and encouragement: Mrs Lu Sinclair, Professor Wong Lai Yoong, Mrs Wong Swee Hoon and Associate Professor Violet Phang. I am indebted to my husband, the immediate members of my family, my relatives, my friends, my readers and all those who in some way or other have encouraged me to carry on writing. A special word of thanks goes to Mr T K Sabapathy for his encouragement. My thanks also go to Professor Ben Farmer at the University of Newcastle, for his foreword to the book.

I wish to express my heartfelt gratitude to Miss Maggie Toy who upon reading my draft manuscript immediately offered me the honour to publish with Academy Group. I am indeed grateful to her for her good advice and her editorial comments.

This book would not have been written if the imperial rulers of the Ming and Qing eras had not concretised their imperial power in the physical form of the classical monuments of Beijing. If these magnificent buildings had been lost, or those that were destroyed not resurrected, the book would not even have materialised, let alone been published. Therefore I wish to acknowledge the imperial rulers for their vision and determination in building and re-building these magnificent buildings, the builders for their dedication in constructing these monuments with such fine details and the conservation workers who have spent years preserving and reconstructing these great buildings. Thanks go to those historians and Chinese scholars who have been contributing to the continuous recording, documenting and developing the sources of Chinese history, architecture and landscape design.

Last but not least, I wish to express my gratitude to Dr Wong Hong Teng, Acting Head, the Department of Chinese Studies, and Ms Tan Sah Mui for helping me to insert the Chinese characters in the text.

Dr Evelyn Lip

All photographs are courtesy of Kenny Lip Yau Sueng.

ABOUT THE AUTHOR:
Dr Evelyn Lip is a chartered architect and a specialist consultant in *feng shui*. During the last twenty-eight years, she has taught architecture in the Universities of Malaysia and Singapore. Dr Lip began her studies in *feng shui* and the metaphysics of architecture in the 1970s, and she has written over thirty books including *Chinese Geomancy* and *Out of China, Culture and Traditions*. Among her talents, she is also a Chinese brush painting artist and she renders the beautiful illustrations featured in all of her books.

COVER: (from above left clockwise) The Dagoba in the Beihai; a half-hipped/half-gabled roof; Fo Xiangge of the Yi Heyuan; a Buddhist temple; roof detail of the Tai Hedian; plan of the Zi Jincheng; bell tower of Bai Masi; exploded structural axonometric; and (centre) jiu, the Chinese character for the number nine.
FRONTISPIECE: The Zhong Hedian of the Gugong

First published in Great Britain in 1995 and reprinted in 1996 by
ACADEMY EDITIONS
An imprint of

ACADEMY GROUP LTD
42 Leinster Gardens, London W2 3AN
Member of the VCH Publishing Group

ISBN 1 85490 427 2

Distributed to the trade in the United States of America by
NATIONAL BOOK NETWORK, INC
4720 Boston Way, Lanham, Maryland 20706

Printed and bound in Singapore

Contents

I am delighted that such a book has been published. Pre-Christian China saw itself as the centre of civilisation and it must be clear to all thinking people that China will move centre-stage again in the twenty-first century.

In geographical terms, China is large, with natural resources, climate and people varying from region to region, and with the buildings of the north having a robustness which contrasts with the more democratic work in the south.

It has been my good fortune to have worked with Evelyn Lip as colleague and co-author in the past decade. She is an eminent and punctilious scholar offering explanation and understanding of subjects, making them clear and establishing their underlying principles.

As ever, architecture is witness to culture, speaking to and for society by bringing messages from the past and making statements about the present, and this rewarding book on Chinese architecture will delight as well as inform scholars.

It is full of insight into basic architectural characteristics, the principles underpinning them, the technology employed in their realisation and the dynastic changes worked upon them and their expression. It shows what continuing importance architecture has to Chinese thinking and offers lessons to us all.

Ben Farmer
Professor of Architecture
University of Newcastle

The Fo Xiangge temple in the Yi Heyuan
is an ideal example of *feng shui* principles,
with its use of powerful colours and
the commanding panorama of the Kun
Minghu in front and hills behind.

Preface

Other learned scholars have written about the tangible aspects of Chinese architecture and landscape but few have given a comprehensive presentation of the intangible aspects. This book is written for Chinese scholars, researchers, architects and those who are interested in all things Chinese.

Therefore, this book aims to examine not only the tangible and functional qualities but also the intangible and metaphysical aspects of some of the most powerful classical buildings and landscape gardens in Beijing and Chengde, China. These buildings and gardens are direct manifestations of the social, cultural and political systems that have spanned the historical past of China for thousands of years from ancient times to the Qing era. They portray the dynamics of the social, cultural, religious and political activities of the most powerful and influential imperial rulers and feudal lords of the Ming and Qing periods.

As early as the third century BC China already assumed itself as the centre of civilisation, placing itself at the centre of the universe. Its classical architecture was indeed a product of its feudalistic systems and it mirrored the supreme power of its rulers. The structural and constructional details based on the beam-frame and bracketing systems reflected its multifaceted cultural traits and highlighted its social organisations. Its harmonious relationship between man and family as well as family and country was seen in the various elements and treatment of architecture. The organisation of spaces in and around building and landscape complexes, expanding from a single unit to a group of structures with courtyards, often reflected the basis and structure of Chinese society.

Chinese emperors were thought to be *tianzi* 天子, the sons of the heavens. They were vested with supreme powers and were treated with utmost dignity, prestige and exaltation. They assumed the role of co-ordinating the seasonal cycles with the cycles of agriculture so that order in nature was assured as the mandate of the heavens. They offered sacrifices during official religious rituals and thus established communication between man and the gods. Emperors played such vital roles as political and religious leaders that their imperial functions had to be held in palaces conceived on the grandest scales and spatial concepts. These power houses were designed and built in the most ornate fashion on sites of good *feng shui*, both scenic and serene. The principles of *feng shui*, the science of creating harmony and balance between the forces of nature and influences of man, play an important role in the creation of the environments of power inhabited by the imperial rulers.

Since the founding of the Qing dynasty (AD 1644–1911) successful endeavours were made to reinforce further the imperial power by concentrating authority into the hands of those who sat on the dragon thrones. Hence, the Forbidden City, sited at the heart of the capital and constructed on 720,000 square metres of land was, indeed, the focal point and the supreme political centre of China. A 160,000-square-metre area of exceptional quality, both in structural and decorative building elements, was provided for imperial administration and residence. The arrangement of interior and exterior spaces, the emphasis on symmetry and balance, as well as the usage of structural and non-structural elements reveal the Chinese concept of space and form with reference to Confucian principles and Taoist ideas. The magnitude of power and the hierarchy of authority were translated into three-dimensional building forms as expressed by the tiers of marble terraces in the great quadrangles of the imperial ground. When homage was paid to the emperor only the high Mandarins and officials were allowed on these terraces. Lower officials were permitted entry to the areas south of the main gateway. Each one had his place and rank in society. Similarly, the emperor must be seen to perform his duties in a manner worthy of his rank. The status of *li* 理 (principle), the existence of *qi* 气 (earth's energy), the balance of the *yin* 阴 (negative) and *yang* 阳 (positive) forces and the harmony of the Five Elements as well as man's relationship with the cosmos, are all manifest in the realm of architecture in the Forbidden City.

The buildings constructed in the Forbidden City accomplish specific intentions and confirm the political as well as the spiritual position of the emperor in China. They represent a repository of imperial power, physically felt and viewed by the rest of the world.

Just as Confucian principles are expressed in the planning of houses, palaces and cities, Taoist philosophy is demonstrated in the landscape of palaces and cities. One of China's ten most scenic landscaped gardens and imperial palace complexes is the Bishu Shanzhuang 避暑山庄 in the foothills of the Yan Shan 燕山 in Chengde 承德. Completed in AD 1792 this splendid mountain resort bears testimony to the grandeur of lifestyle and the supremacy of the political powers of the Qing emperor who built it as his summer retreat, where he would remain in residence from April to October of each year. Enriched by luxurious and splendid furnishing the imperial palaces were decorated by the most skilful artisans and craftsmen, while the imperial libraries were furnished with the most valuable collections of book and art works.

Similarly, the Yi Heyuan 颐和园, the Summer Palace in the northwestern suburbs of Beijing, built for the retirement of the empress dowager, Cixi 慈禧, was adorned with precious jewels, exquisite works of fine art and pottery and finished with the best building materials that give a symbolic notion in physical form which could be seen and felt. Covering an area of 290 hectares, it was built on the most scenic site with hills to the rear, huge lakes in front and all the features of an excellent *feng shui* model, enhanced by man-made as well as natural features and endowed with natural beauty. Its buildings, palaces, temples and pavilions were placed in such a way that harmony and balance were achieved and the energy of the earth was captured and retained. Its *feng shui* was splendid. The supremacy of the empress must have been pervasive when she gave audience to her ministers at her courts built on a raised dais, and the throne furnished with exquisitely carved screens and furniture.

Religion was used to enhance the spiritual leadership of the emperor who was believed to possess innate powers which he could use to seek favours from the gods more effectively than his subjects. Being the supreme arbiter of power and prosperity, great temples, such as the Temple of Heaven and the Altar of Heaven, were constructed for him to pray for good harvests and blessings from his ancestors.

This book is not meant to give a comprehensive history of imperial China. Therefore, only short introductions on the historical and religious background are given in Chapters 1 to 3. Since it is written for architects and students of architecture the general characteristics of traditional architecture in China are given in Chapter 4 under various headings such as environment, planning, construction, roof form and decoration, colour scheme, walls, windows and ceilings.

Beijing, the seat of Chinese government as early as the Yuan era, once again became the capital city during the Ming and Qing dynasties because of the shift of the communication network and dynastic need. The imperial palaces, being the heart and nerve centre, were purposely planned so as to confirm the incarnation of the supreme imperial power. An attempt is made in Chapter 5 to describe the general features of this great city.

The most important group of historical and classical buildings in Beijing is the Gugong. Therefore, a detailed description of the layout and metaphysical aspects of planning and design are presented in Chapters 6 and 7. Chapter 7 gives the very basis of the design concept; the theory of the *yin* and *yang* of *kanyu*, the Chinese art of placement with reference to the metaphysical theories of the working of the Five Elements and the Jiuxing system of *feng shui*. These theories formulate the principles and roots of Chinese planning and architecture.

The Qing emperors, being regarded as descendants of the heavenly gods, were responsible for conducting the worship of the gods on a national level. Splendidly built temples of magnificent scale were therefore constructed for the worship of the heavens by the emperors. In Chapter 8 the Temple of Heaven and other glorious temples are described in detail and illustrated with colour images and drawings.

A Chinese city was often planned in a series of concentric rectangles enclosed by walls and relieved by lakes, hills, valleys, gardens, courtyards and parks. The built and natural environments were always appropriately planned to augur good energy and landscaped according to intuitive Taoist ideas of *yin* and *yang*, void and solid, water and hill and so on. The magnificent Ming and Qing landscaped imperial gardens, the Yi Heyuan and the Bishu Shanzhuang, are thus described in Chapter 9.

Throughout the text where Chinese words have been romanized, following the Mandarin (pinyin) pronunciation, they are followed by Chinese founts. The use of pinyin alone would be misleading and insufficient to give the correct meaning of these words as many Chinese characters with very different connotations can sound similar when transcribed in Mandarin. The Chinese fount, therefore, ensures the correct translation.

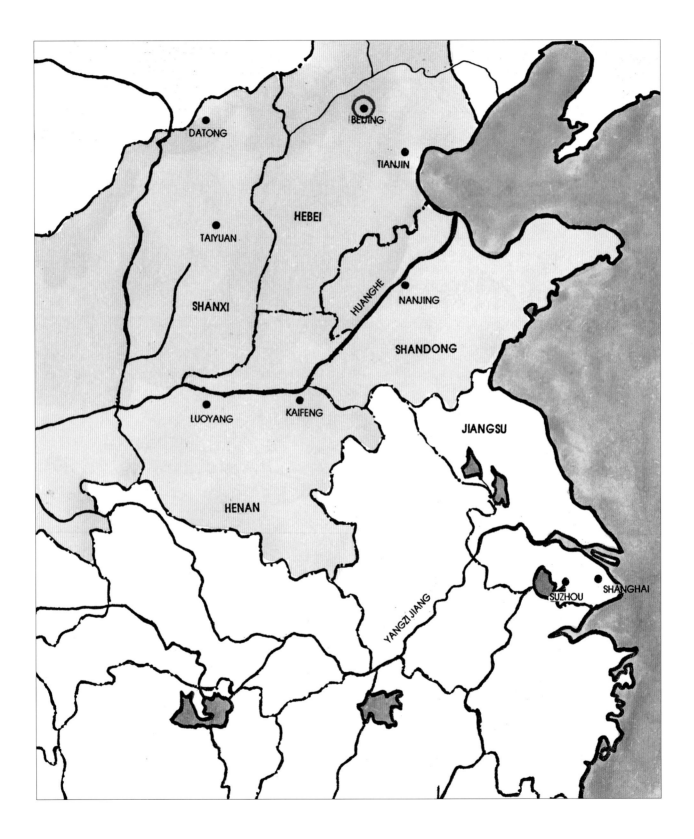

A Brief History of China

China is a large country with a population of over one thousand million. Its historical past is richly embedded with cultural, political and social changes. For over five thousand years its religious practices, social order, architectural and philosophical thinking have not changed drastically. Its historical development can be traced to the dawn of civilisation. China entered into a period of agriculture and domestication at about 2,500 BC during the rule of the Wudi 武帝, the mystical emperors, Huang Di 皇帝, Zhuan Zu 颛诅, Di Ku 帝喾, Yao 尧 and Shun 舜, who were well known for their wisdom during the period 2,550–2,140 BC. Yao united his people and brought about harmony; Shun deepened the rivers to control floods.

During the Spring and Autumn period (770–476 BC) and the Xia 夏 era (twenty-first to sixteenth century BC) emperor Yu 禹 was noted for his contribution in controlling floods and improving the irrigation systems.[1] The emperor of the Shang 商 dynasty, (sixteenth to eleventh century BC) was known for his building of cities in many parts of China.[2] Succeeding the Shang ruler was Wu Wang who overthrew Yin Shang 殷商 to start a new era of Zhou 周.(1066–771 BC was known as West Zhou 西周 and 770–221 BC was known as East Zhou 东周.) During the East Zhou philosophers such as Confucius and Lao Zi 老子 started schools of thought which later became powerful cultural and religious institutions. The Zhou rulers not only brought the system of government to maturity but also divided the ranking of feudal lords into grades.[3] In 841 BC a rebellion drove the tenth emperor of Zhou, Li Wang 厉王, into exile. The Zhou dynasty was recovered in 788 BC but seventeen years later the emperor lost control and the country was ruled by the feudal lords.[4] The capital was moved to Luoyang. Following this era a period of uncertainty prevailed as the warlords fought for power during the Warring States 三国 (403–221 BC).

China was unified by Qinshi Huangdi 秦始皇帝 after he had established the Qin 秦 dynasty in 221 BC.[5] Although Qinshi Huangdi ruled with an iron hand, he contributed much progress in terms of building and construction. He also organised China into a hierarchy of counties and prefectures under governmental control. He commissioned large-scale irrigation works, extensive construction works and in 214 BC, the 3,000 kilometre Great Wall was built to defend the country against attacks by the Mongolians.

Qinshi Huangdi was succeeded by his second son, Er Shi 二世, who was overthrown by Liu Bang 刘邦 or Han Gaodi 汉高帝, who established the Han 汉 dynasty. (West Han 西汉 was from BC 206–AD 23 and East Han 东汉 from AD 25–220.) During Gaodi's rule internal conflicts and fighting led the emperor's advisor to move the capital to Changan 长安. The fourth emperor of Han, Wen Di 文帝, was a wise ruler who improved the welfare of his people and the economy of the country.

The Han emperors not only constructed huge palaces and cities but also started institutions of music. Wu Di 武帝 (140–87 BC) was one of the more dynamic emperors during that era. He ordered the maintenance of extensive water controls to sustain the success of agriculture and he initiated the imperial examination system. He spent fifty years fighting the nomads, overthrew the rebels and won many battles. Buddhism

Sketch map of northern China

was brought into China from India during the Han dynasty and was developed hand in hand with Taoism 道教 and Confucianism.[6] The Han kingdom was overthrown by Toba Wei who set up his capital in Luoyang in AD 494 and occupied northern China.

In AD 595 a dreadful famine struck northern China. Yang Jian 杨坚 led his men and evacuated Changan. In AD 581 the north and south were unified by Yang Jian, the Sui 隋 ruler. Yang Jian was assassinated and succeeded by his son, Yang Di 炀帝 who built his capital at Luoyang. Yang Di built the Grand Canal stretching from Beijing to Hangzhou, but his foreign policy made him extremely unpopular and he was assassinated and succeeded briefly by his nephew, Gong Di 恭帝. The Sui kingdom (AD 581–618) was put to an end in AD 618 by Li Yuan who established the Tang 唐 dynasty and built his capitals at Changan 长安 and Luoyang 洛阳. Known as Gao Zu 高祖, Li Yuan was succeeded by his son, Li Shimin 李世民 or Tai Zong 太宗, who did much to unify the kingdom. Tai Zong emerged as an able political leader and China was known as an economic power in Asia. Art and literature flourished under his leadership. He was succeeded by Tang Gaozong 唐高宗. After the death of Gaozong, China was ruled by the empress Wu Zetian 武则天 who was not popular but noted for her promotion of poetry and literature. The Tang dynasty was in a state of turmoil in the tenth century AD and was succeeded by the Song 宋 dynasty (AD 960–1279). During this era a significant architectural treatise, the *Yingzao Fashi* 营造法式 written by Li Jie, was published.

The period that separated the Tang and the Song was known as the Wudai (Five Dynasties, namely the Hou Liang 后梁, the Hou Tang 后唐, the Hou Jin 后晋, the Hou Han 后汉 and the Hou Zhou 后周). The first North Song emperor, Tai Zu 太祖, organised his administration fairly well. He was succeeded by Tai Zong 太宗. Altogether nine emperors ruled the North Song era (AD 960–1279) and another nine ruled the South Song dynasty (AD 1127–1279). The Song periods were the most culturally flourishing eras. Chinese brush painting was promoted by Hui Zong 徽宗 (AD 1101–1125), the eighth emperor of the North Song, who was a brush painter himself. Literature and art were promoted and, simultaneously, the seafarer's compass and gunpowder were invented. Mongolian and Tartar tribes invaded the Song kingdom and the ruling government had to abandon the capital at Kaifeng 开封 and move to Hangzhou 杭州. A period of turmoil ensued and China fell into the hands of the Liao 辽 who were later defeated by the Manchurians who began the Jin 金 dynasty. The Chinese kingdom was conquered by Kublai Khan, the grandson of Genghis Khan, who established the Yuan 元 dynasty (AD 1279–1368). The Mongol capital was set up in Beijing. The Grand Canal was completed and European traders were therefore able to reach the major cities.

The Mongolians were unpopular and after a period of unrest they were overthrown in a revolt led by Zhu Yuanzhang 朱元璋 who founded the Ming 明 dynasty (AD 1368–1644). In AD 1399 the first Ming emperor passed away and the throne was succeeded by his grandson, Hui Di 惠帝. But four years later, Hui Di's uncle led a revolt and declared himself emperor Cheng Zu 成祖. In AD 1421 emperor Cheng Zu moved his capital to Beijing and the Forbidden City, the Zi Jincheng 紫禁城, was laid out and enclosed with high walls. During this period the construction of one of China's great palace complexes in the Forbidden City was started. Completed by the Qing 清 emperor, the successor of the Ming rulers, it was based on the concept of symmetry, with all its principal buildings and gateways facing south. Enclosed by a moat and waterway that was taken from the Beihai 北海 (north sea) its buildings were ventilated by courtyards. The production of Ming 'blue and white' porcelain flourished, but corruption and extravagance led to the Ming government's downfall.

Rebels under the leadership of Li Zicheng 李自成 seized Luoyang where the food supply was kept. Li marched into Beijing. However, Wu Sangui 吴三桂, one of the officials of the Ming administration, was against Li. He collaborated with the Manchurians and opened the gate at Shan Haiguan 山海关. Seizing the opportunity of a power vacuum in Beijing the Manchurians installed Shun Zhi as the first emperor of the Qing dynasty and the Ming dynasty fell to the Manchurians.

During the Qing period (AD 1644–1911) the *Goncheng Zuofa Celie*, a well presented, well written book on constructional methods and technical details for building was published. The outstanding Qing rulers, Kang Xi 康熙 (AD 1662–1723) and Qian Long 乾隆 (AD 1736–1796), both promoted Chinese culture and adopted Chinese administration. But towards the end of the Qing era the kingdom was in the hands of weak rulers who had to concede to increased trade with the British. The objection to opium imports led to the Opium War in AD 1839. Unrest arose and the Taiping Rebellion took place in AD 1850. The Qing government was weak and corrupt, and was put to an end in AD 1911 by the Guo Mindang 国民党 (the Nationalists) when the empress dowager signed an abdication document on behalf of the last emperor, Pu Yi 溥仪. Under the leadership of Sun Zongshan 孙中山 China was ruled by the Nationalists who were supposed to be in alliance with the Communists. However, a year later, Yuan Shikai 袁世凯 tried to restore the Qing monarchy, but in vain. Sun Zongshan passed away in AD 1925, to be succeeded by Jiang Kaishi 蒋介石. The capital was moved to Nanjing when Beijing was captured in AD 1928 by the Nationalists. At this point, the Communists split with the Nationalists and fought against them. They marched from Jiangxi Province to Shanxi Province under the leadership of Mao Zedong 毛泽东 and established their headquarters at Yunnan 云南.

In April 1949 the Communists or the People's Liberation Army, under the leadership of Mao Zedong won the final victory, defeated the Nationalists and declared China the People's Republic of China. The capital was re-established in Beijing and China was governed along the Socialist system. Significant industries and business centres were nationalised and agricultural ventures were centralised. In AD 1958 the Great Leap Forward was implemented so that people's communities were established to encourage innovation and leadership. Eight years later, the Cultural Revolution followed to reinforce the idea of reform and revolution. As a result, disruption and chaos took place. However, by 1970, order and calm were restored.

Mao Zedong passed away in AD 1970 and was succeeded by Hua Guofeng 华国锋. Deng Xiaoping 邓小平 was given the vice-chairmanship in AD 1977. Under Deng's leadership industrialisation accelerated and the economy grew rapidly. In AD 1980 Hua Guofeng was succeeded by Hu Yaobang 胡耀邦 as chairman of China. Hu was succeeded by Jiang Zeming 江泽明 in AD 1989.

China is now a fast developing country, achieving rapid economic growth.

Notes

1 Prior to the establishment of the Xia period the throne was not passed to the next emperor by birth right as each was chosen by merit.

2 The Shang rulers left written records cast in bronze or inscribed on tortoise shells.

3 See the *Shijing* 诗经, the Book of Odes, op cit, on feudalism during the Zhou era.

4 See the *Shujing*, the Book of History, op cit, and *Liji* 礼记, the Book of Rites. In the seventh century BC there were two hundred feudal territories.

5 Qinshi Huangdi united seven states and united China. He divided the country into thirty-six provinces, each administered by a governor. Each province was divided into several counties.

6 Refer to the short introductions on Buddhism, Taoism and Confucianism on pp15-16. Other philosophies such as Maoism and Legalism also evolved during that era but their influences soon vanished. Taoism and Confucianism developed into religious beliefs.

The Religious History of China

Traditionally, the Chinese have always been dedicated to ancestor worship and to the three major religious doctrines: Buddhism, Taoism and Confucianism unless they belong to other faiths such as Islam or Christianity. The Taoist or even Buddhist followers may not adhere strictly to any one of the religions. Many Chinese, especially those who live in rural areas, worship numerous gods.[1] They embrace both Buddhism and Taoism, and such religious pluralism emerges as Syncretism.

Strictly speaking, ancestor worship is not a religion. It is, rather, a way of paying respect to ancestors especially during Qing Ming 清明 (All Souls Day). The Chinese choose burial grounds for their ancestors carefully, determining that they are not affected by dampness or insect attack, to ensure the well-being of the dead.

Confucianism is closely related to ancestor worship as it was started by Confucius 孔夫子 who preached filial piety and respect for elders during the fifth century BC. For Confucius the ceremony of ancestor worship was merely the meeting between the *yin* (spiritual) and the *yang* (material) worlds. Good fortunes would be bestowed on the dutiful children who gave respect and love to their parents.

Born in 551 BC, Confucius came from the state of Lu 鲁, Shandong 山东. During the Spring and Autumn period (772–481 BC) the Zhou dynasty had lost its powerful rule over the feudal leaders. Confucius became a clerk in the temple of the Duke of Zhou where he learnt the rituals of ceremonies held in the temple. He became an expert of these rituals with many followers. Throughout his life Confucius taught a social order based on love for one's fellow men and respect for one's country and authority. The main theme of his teaching centred on perfect virtue, humanity, benevolence, tolerance, courtesy, magnanimity, faith and diligence. He based his social order on a feudal ethic which expected the emperor to behave with benevolence and love for his people so that justice could be enjoyed by his subjects. When the ruler exerted oppression instead of benevolence the mandate of heaven would be withdrawn and he would be overthrown.

In 502 BC Confucius was given the post of Secretary of Justice. But his idealistic intentions could not be realised so he resigned and travelled for a period of fourteen years until he reached the age of sixty-seven. He then retired to Lu and edited five Classics: the *Shijing* 诗经 (the Book of Odes), the *Liji* (the Book of Rites), the *Shiji* 史记 (the Book of History), the *Chunqiu* 春秋 (the Annals of Spring and Autumn) and the *Yijing* 易经 (the Book of Changes). Confucius passed away at the age of seventy-two; he was buried at Lu.

Taoism was founded by Lao Zi 老子, a philosopher born in 604 BC in Henan. A recluse during the early part of his life, he became a curator at the royal court of the Zhou ruler. He taught man to follow the laws of nature. His fundamental doctrines were recorded in the *Dao Dijing* (a Classic on the Nature of Earth).

Taoism was a way of thinking and did not become a religion until Zhang Daoling 张道陵 initiated a movement that incorporated sorcery into the belief in AD 142 in Sichuan 四川. Zhang established a school in Sichuan 四川 on the teaching of Taoism.

A Confucian temple
A Buddhist temple

All those who followed Zhang had to contribute five *dou* 五斗 (box) of rice. They addressed Zhang as Tian Shi 天师 (Heavenly Teacher) and Lao Zi as Taishang Laojun 太上老君 (Wise Sage of Supreme Level). The main Taoist Classic was *Dao Dijing*. It was believed that man could be trained to become immortal and thus Taoism became a popular religion.[2] Huge Taoist temples were constructed.

In AD 317 Ge Hong 葛洪 synthesised Taoist philosophy and Chinese ethics. In the fifth century AD Guan Yinzi 关尹子 updated the Taoist doctrines. Lu Xiujing 陆修静 at Lushan edited the Taoist Classics named *Sandong Jingshu*. In AD 1167 at Shandong 山东 Jin Dading 金大定 and Huang Chongyang initiated a fresh approach to practising Taoism and attracted many followers.

The main features of Taoism are:
- Taoism is divided into two schools of thought, northern and southern;
- the ethics of Taoism include patience, harmony, simplicity and contentment;
- Taoism encourages the belief in divination and usage of charms;
- Taoism encourages the embrace of many gods such as the Jade Emperor 玉皇大帝, Guan Yin 观音 the Goddess of Mercy, gods of Literature, Wealth, Longevity and Fortune.

Buddhism originated in India and was founded in the sixth century BC by Siddhartha Gautama (later known as Sakyamuni) who was an Indian prince. He gave up his life of luxury to search for ways of overcoming suffering and the pains of ageing and dying. At the age of twenty-nine he left his wife, family and kingdom in search of enlightenment. After a period of six years of tremendous effort and experience of all forms of physical self-sacrifice he attained enlightenment at the foot of a bodhi tree. He had many followers to carry out his teachings, listed as follows:
- misery was part of one's life and existence;
- every form of desire caused anxiety and possibly suffering;
- when desire was eliminated suffering was overcome;
- desire might be overcome through the eight paths to Nirvana, a state of perfect peace and freedom from suffering;
- the eight paths of Nirvana were achieved by modifying one's feelings, actions, speech, memory and meditation.

About one hundred years after the death of the Buddha his followers founded two schools namely the Theravada and the Sarvastivada. Buddha's followers observe the five principles of Buddhism which are:
- not to slay that which has life;
- not to steal;
- not to be lustful;
- not to be light in conversation;
- not to drink alcoholic drinks.

Buddhism originated in India where it became popular with the support of King Kaniska in the second century. It was later brought to China, southeast Asia and other countries. After it was introduced into China it flourished during the rule of Ming Di 明帝 of the East Han dynasty (in the year AD 67). Many Buddhist temples were built and, by the Nanbei period (AD 420–589), two thousand eight hundred and forty-six Buddhist temples and fifty-two thousand and seven hundred monasteries had been constructed.[3] Buddhism flourished further during the Tang dynasty (AD 618–907). Sutras were translated and monks were sent out of China to India to obtain more scriptures from the west. However, in the ninth century AD Buddhism suffered a set back as the emperor was not in favour of the religion and ordered many of the Buddhist temples to be demolished.

By the thirteenth century AD Buddhism had declined but was revived in the nineteenth century. Many Buddhist centres were established to spread the teaching of Buddha. It continues to be practised in China, southeast Asia and other South Pacific regions.

In a Buddhist temple, the main altar houses the icons of the Buddha, Guan Yin and, frequently, the Eighteen Arhats or other Bodhisattvas who delayed their salvation in order to remain in the world to assist man to achieve spiritual enlightenment. Guan Yin, the Goddess of Mercy, is worshipped in both Buddhist and Taoist temples.

Notes

1 The Chinese used to pray to the moon, the sun, the sky, the earth and the stars. As early as the Shun period, about three thousand years ago, they believed in many gods. See *Chen Meng Jia* 陈梦家, Yin Xu Bu Zi Zong Shu 殷墟卜辞综述 (Japan) 1964, p562.

2 Zhang Daoling dramatically acquired immortality in AD 156 when he disappeared. See Cotterell, Arthur, *China, A Concise Cultural History*, John Murray (London) 1988, p120.

3 See Ren Jiyu 任继愈, op cit, p62. In the 'Records of the Buddhist Countries' the development of Mahayana Buddhism in China is given. It describes how the Buddhist monk, Fa Xian 法显, travelled to India to receive scriptures.

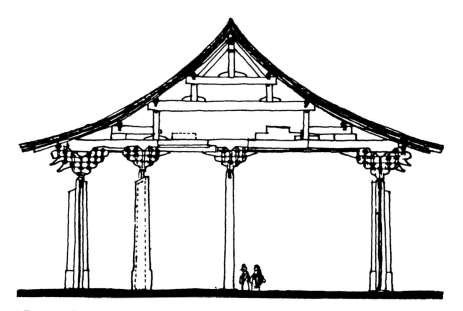

A Taoist temple

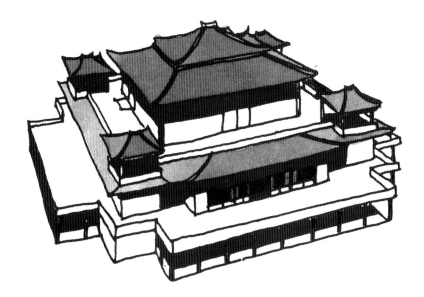

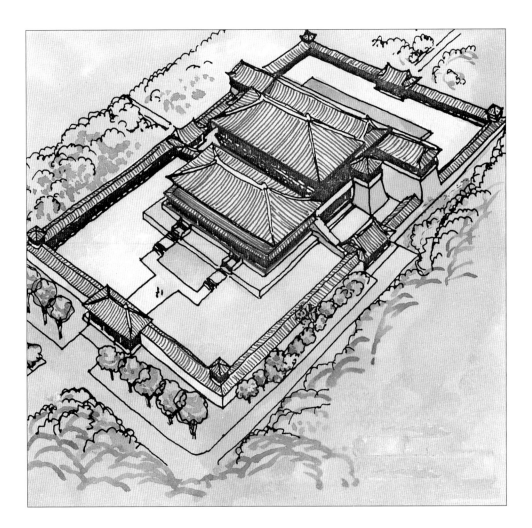

Architectural Development

Architectural development in China is deeply rooted in her history. During the Stone Age the Chinese lived in caves or timber structures called *chao* as recorded in the *Wudu* 五蠹 (written in the Warring States, 403–221 BC). Imperial rulers had the choice of alternating their places of accommodation from cave-like dwellings in winter to *chao* dwellings in summer.[1] In the ancient classics *Kao Gongji* 考工记 dated 481 BC it is recorded that dwellings had hipped roofs.

Shang dynasty writing was the earliest to be based on graphic and symbolic representation.[2] From these writings it is evident that during this period buildings were of post and beam construction and some were raised above ground. The design of structures was tailored to the needs of the users. From the engraved bronzewares of the Shang and Zhou eras came the knowledge that symbols were used to express the aspirations of the people.[3] During the Western Zhou period *banwa* and *tongwa* (tiles still used at present) were already used for roofs.[4] During the Chunqiu era (eighth century BC) one of China's most skilled craftsmen, Lu Ban 鲁班, had already created fine tools for building.[5]

When Qinshi Huangdi united China he mobilised all the labourers and prisoners to construct the infrastructures of cities and huge palaces.[6]

Following the footsteps of Qin the succeeding West Han rulers continued to construct huge complexes. These palaces, complete with gardens, were of a scale far superior to those built in the earlier eras.[7]

Porcelain of the Han dynasty reveals that the Han developed a few types of timber-framed courtyard houses. *Dougong* 斗拱 or timber brackets had also been developed as is evident from engravings on bronze wares dated during the West Han period.

According to a number of scholars there were three main high points in the development of Chinese architecture.[8] The first was found to be from the Qin (221–206 BC) to the Han (206 BC–AD 220) periods, in which the palaces of Qinshi Huangdi 秦始皇帝, the Xian Yanggong 咸阳宫 and the A Fanggong 阿房宫, were built to a scale and finish that surpassed all precedents.[9] The Han rulers had the Wei Yanggong 未央宫, the Chang Legong 长乐宫 rebuilt and the Beigong 北宫 constructed in timber and in the traditional style. The basic roof forms such as the hipped, the gabled and the pyramidal, were used to cover buildings. Roof ridges were mainly straight and included roof ornaments on the ridges.[10]

Columns were round, square and some were eight-sided. Buildings were set up on podiums, of which some were engraved with patterns.[11]

During the Nanbei Chao 南北朝 (AD 420–589) the architectural detailing was rather crude but innovative. Roof ridges were terminated with curved-up *wen* 吻.[12] Column bases were developed as well as other details for windows and doors.[13]

The second peak in the development of Chinese architecture stretched from the Sui (AD 581–618) to the Song (AD 960–1279) eras. This development accompanied the flourishing of the Buddhist faith in China. Indian influence contributed to the maturity of pagodas (some fashioned after the stupa design) and cave architecture.

Chart showing pictographs of Shang Dynasty:

jing	京	capital city
shi	室	room/interior of building
gong	宫	palace
gao	高	tall
qin	寝	sleep
zhai	宅	house
niu	牛	ox
men	门	door
jia	家	home/family
kun	困	imprison

A Han dynasty building complex
The Lin Dedian of Da Minggong

Wave pattern

Phoenix pattern

Dragon pattern

Square pattern

The main theme in the development focused on the harmony of materials and the proportional relationship of building elements.[14]

This period reached its peak when Li Jie 李诚 wrote the *Yingzao Fashi* which was published during the Song dynasty. The *Yingzao Fashi*, which contains traditional Chinese methods of construction and detailing, remains a handbook of Chinese architecture for scholars and craftsmen. Even though the scale of the buildings erected during the Song was less significant than that of the Tang, the detailing was much more complex and rich in variety.[15] The Liaos inherited the Tang style of building enabling the bracketing system of construction to evolve fully.

The third phase and the last high point in the development of traditional Chinese architecture was during the Ming (AD 1368–1644) and Qing (AD 1644–1911) dynasties. It was during this period that huge palace complexes, landscaped garden complexes and religious complexes were constructed to a scale and grandeur surpassing all previous precedents.[16] The monuments built remain to the present day; the Gugong or Palace Museum in Beijing is one of the world's finest examples.

The most significant developments during these periods were: the bracketing system, which became streamlined and the columns more elegant; the more obvious terminating features of the roof; and the increased number of roof ornaments on the roof corners. Other building elements such as doors, windows and balustrades also evolved and changed slightly. For example, the *mending* had become purely decorative instead of a detailing device to hide the joints. Decorative motifs became even richer than ever.[17]

The development of the construction system introduced since the Tang dynasty has not changed in principle but has evolved in detail. This is because China has long been governed by rulers who adopted the feudal system with its pre-determined building requirements and styles. Building scale and size, planning and concepts of space, constructional and structural detailing, usage of materials and decorative themes for a dynasty were decided and executed in accordance to the edicts of the feudal system of the preceding dynasties. The architectural detailing was developed to some extent but the overall style was constrained by traditional practices. Even through succeeding dynasties and the replacement of capital cities, the basic concepts of architecture, planning and construction remained constant; the beam-frame construction incorporating *dougong* bracketing prevailed.

Basic traditional Chinese planning both before and since the Tang dynasty is based on the courtyard concept,[18] while the structural system is based on the beam-frame system.[19] However, the size and detailing of the *dougong* have evolved from large to small in proportion with the overall height of the column.[20] Various roof forms have also been used since the Han dynasty until the present day. The same can be said for the colour scheme, usage of materials and application of decorative motifs.

Although few significant changes occur in the style of classical architecture, there are significant differences between the roof design of a traditional building in the north and that of one in the south of China. This is most evident in the design of the main ridge and the corner rib of the roof. Generally, the roof ridge of a traditional building in the north is straight as are the corner ribs to a certain extent, whereas the roof ridge found in the south is curved and the corner ribs tilt upward prominently. This is determined by many reasons, including aesthetic and cultural traits.[21]

Notes

1 See Li Yun 礼运 in the *Liji* 礼记, Confucian Classics. Evidence of this was discovered in the archaeological discovery at Xian.

2 Refer to the chart of Chinese pictographs written on tortoise shells. The pictographs depict the types of plan required to serve the specific purposes.

3 See Zhang Weichi 张维持, *Yinzhou Qingtong Qitong Lun* 殷周铜器通论 Kexue Chuban She 科学出版社, (China) 1958, pp102-120.

4 See *Zhongguo Kexue Yuankao Guyan Jiusuo* 中国科学院考古研究所, Kexue Chuban She 科学出版社, (China) 1959.

5 See *Mozi* 墨子 Section 13, and *Mengzi* 孟子 Section 7. Lu Ban was a native of the state of Lu who lived during the Chunqiu period. He was well known for his superb craftsmanship and for his creation of wooden tools for timber construction.

6 See *Shiji* 史记, Qinshi Huang Benji 秦始皇本记 Section 6.

7 See Liu Dunzhen 刘敦桢, *Zhongguo Gudai Jianzhu Shi* 中国古代建筑史, Zhongguo Jianzhu Gongye Chuban She 中国建筑 工业出版社, (Beijing) 1980, p41. The emperor of West Han rebuilt the Wei Yanggong 未央宫, the Chang Legong 长乐宫 and the Beigong 北宫 before he constructed the new palaces.

8 See Cheng Wanli 程万里, *Zhongguo Chuantong Jianzhu* 中国传统建筑, Zhongguo Jianzhu Gongye Chuban She 中国建筑工业出版社, (Hong Kong) 1991, p7.

9 See *Shiji* 史记 Confucian Classics, section on Qinshi Huang Benji 秦始皇本纪. It states that more than seventy thousand labourers constructed the A Fanggong while they were prisoners of the Qin administration.

10 Wei Yanggong was built on a huge podium. See Li Qianlang 李乾郎, *Jianzhu* 建筑, Youshi Wenfa Shiye Gongshi 幼狮文化事业公司, (Taipei) 1986, p71. Also see Cheng Wanli 程万里 op cit, p42. Refer to the drawing of a Han dynasty building complex within Changan 长安 city.

11 Records of such podiums were found in Shandong.

12 This can be seen on the Gu Yangdong 古阳洞 in Luoyang 洛阳.

13 Drawings of such columns were found in caves.

14 Da Yanta 大雁塔 demonstrates harmonious proportions on its facade. Refer to the drawing of the Sui dynasty Lin Dedian 麟德殿 of Da Minggong 大明宫.

15 Refer to the roof terminating details of the *wenshou* 吻兽 of the Du Lesi 独乐寺 at Jixian 蓟县 which dates back to the Song dynasty.

16 The Qing emperors constructed huge palaces and large-scale gardens far superior to those of their predecessors. Empress dowager, Cixi 慈禧 was very extravagant. Her imperial kitchen was so large that it had eight courtyards and consisted of one hundred and twenty-eight kitchens for preparing various types of food for her.

17 The caissons of the various palaces built during the Ming and Qing dynasties in the Zi Jincheng were exquisitely detailed and built. The famous Changlang at the Yi Heyuan was designed with ornate details and the beams vividly painted.

18 Refer to the sketch of the Lin Dedian on previous page and note the courtyard concept being adopted.

19 See illustrations on pp22, 30.

20 See illustrations on pp26, 30.

21 See Lip, Evelyn, *Chinese Temple Architecture in Singapore*, unpublished PhD thesis, National University of Singapore, 1984, pp15-39. One hundred and fifty Chinese temples in Singapore were studied and their origins were traced. It was found that the traditional buildings were modelled upon their precedents in south China. The tilted-up roof ridges and corner ribs had their origin in temples in south China.

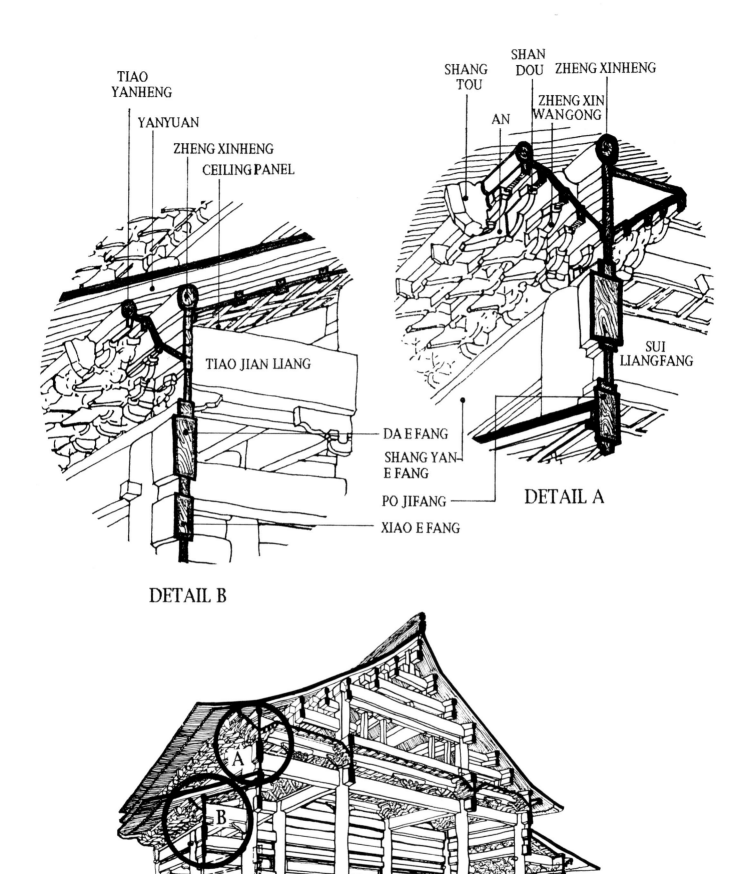

TIAO YANHENG

YANYUAN

ZHENG XINHENG

CEILING PANEL

TIAO JIAN LIANG

DA E FANG

SHANG YAN E FANG

PO JIFANG

XIAO E FANG

DETAIL B

SHANG TOU

SHAN DOU

ZHENG XINHENG

AN

ZHENG XIN WANGONG

SUI LIANGFANG

DETAIL A

A

B

Characteristics of Traditional Chinese Architecture

Chinese architecture is most unique in terms of planning, construction and the application of decorative motifs as well as its long historical development. Already invented during the East Zhou dynasty was the bracketing system employing a bearing block to support brackets. As early as the Qin dynasty (third century BC) magnificent palaces were built at Xianyang 咸阳. After Qinshi Huangdi 秦始皇帝 had conquered the other kingdoms and united China as one nation, the A Fanggong 阿房宫 and the Li Shanling 骊山陵 were built, which were considered architectural feats at the time. Structural works included the building of the Great Wall, the deepening of the canals and the building of dams. During the Han dynasty the bracketing system was developed further.

In the Three Kingdom period many religious buildings were constructed by the Wei warlords. The Wei kingdom alone included as many as one thousand three hundred and sixty-seven monasteries.[1] Architecture flourished further during the Sui dynasty (sixth century AD). By the Tang dynasty (seventh century AD) the capital was moved to Changan, and Luoyang was the second most important major city in China. The first Buddhist temple, Bai Masi 白马寺, was built in Luoyang in AD 67. The most notable architectural publication of the Song dynasty (AD 960–1101) was the *Yingzao Fashi* 营造法式 written by Li Jie 李诚. The Ming emperor moved his capital to Beijing and started to build the imperial palaces at the Zi Jincheng 紫禁城 (the Forbidden City) in AD 1420. The most notable treatise on landscape architecture published during the Ming era was the *Yuan Yi* 园冶 and, in the Qing dynasty, the *Gongpu Gongcheng Zuofa* 工部工程做法 recorded constructional methods. It was published in AD 1734 and continues to be the reference for skilled craftsmen and builders.

Chinese architectural characteristics can be described and classified into the following: built environment, planning, construction, bracketing system, roof form, roof section, roof decorations, colour scheme, walls, columns, tiles, windows, doors and openings, podiums and balustrades.

Built Environment

Since ancient times the surrounding environment and its effects on a building have been very important to the Chinese. It has long been established that the building must be sited and constructed to be in harmony with the natural setting of the site to maximise the benefits the site can offer. The ancients called this aspect of environmental design *xiang di* 相地 which is now called *kanyu* or *feng shui* 风水.[2]

Every building or building complex has to be designed with reference to the *yin* and *yang* elements on or around the site. The left of the building complex is *yang* and is associated with the heavenly forces, while the right, *yin*, is associated with the earth's energy. The ancestor shrine and bell tower are placed on the left and the temple for deities and drum tower are on the right.

Construction details of structural elements of the Tai Hedian of the Gugong

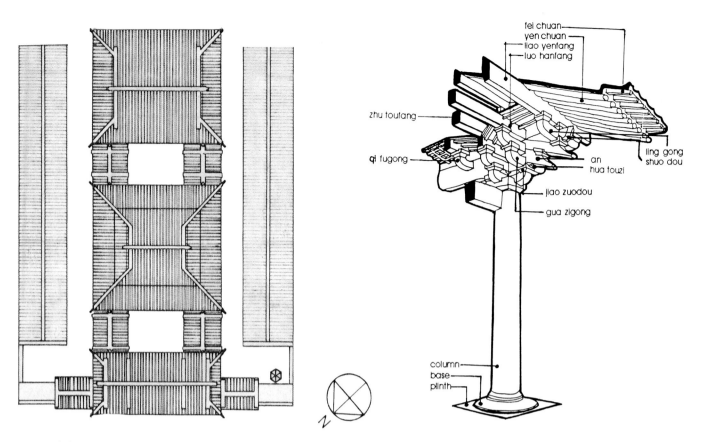

A courtyard plan

Details showing the relationship of the structural elements of a Chinese building

Labels in the detail drawing:
- fei chuan
- yen chuan
- liao yenfang
- luo hanfang
- zhu toufang
- qi fugong
- an hua touzi
- ling gong shuo dou
- jiao zuodou
- gua zigong
- column base plinth

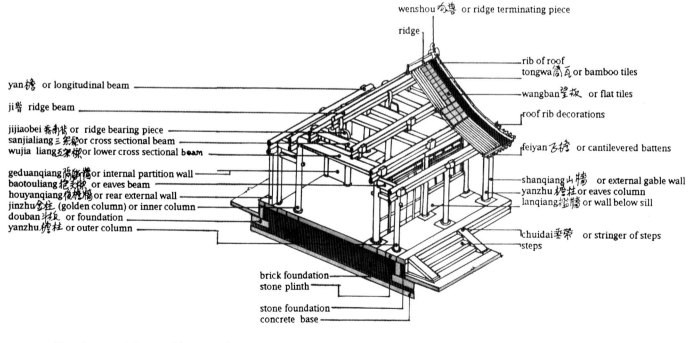

- wenshou 吻兽 or ridge terminating piece
- ridge
- rib of roof
- tongwa 筒瓦 or bamboo tiles
- wangban 望板 or flat tiles
- roof rib decorations
- feiyan 飞檐 or cantilevered battens
- shanqiang 山墙 or external gable wall
- yanzhu 檐柱 or eaves column
- lanqiang 槛墙 or wall below sill
- chuidai 垂带 or stringer of steps
- steps

- yan 檩 or longitudinal beam
- ji 脊 ridge beam
- jijiaobei 脊角背 or ridge bearing piece
- sanjialiang 三架梁 or cross sectional beam
- wujia liang 五架梁 or lower cross sectional beam
- geduanqiang 隔断墙 or internal partition wall
- baotouliang 抱头梁 or eaves beam
- houyanqiang 后檐墙 or rear external wall
- jinzhu 金柱 (golden column) or inner column
- douban 斗板 or foundation
- yanzhu 檐柱 or outer column

- brick foundation
- stone plinth
- stone foundation
- concrete base

Three-dimensional drawing of the structural post, roof, wall and foundation

Planning

The courtyard has always played a significant role in Chinese architecture as it serves the multiple purposes of providing privacy, ventilation and light. The number of courtyards within a building and the accompanying sense of privacy and space reflect the importance of the building and the social status of the occupants.[3] This concept has not changed over the centuries and is adopted from the north to the south of China, classified as follows:

- the concept of *si heyuan* 四合院 making a courtyard concept like the word *ri* 日 based on symmetry, axial planning, north/south orientation and walled enclosure;
- the concept of *san heyuan* 三合院 making a courtyard concept like the word *kou* 口 based on symmetry, and axial planning but without north/south orientation or walled enclosure; and
- the concept of 'L' or 'I' formation with a front courtyard.

Chinese plans may be rectangular, square, round or a combination of geometric shapes.[4] The main hall along the axial line is named the *mingtang* 明堂. The side halls are called the *xiangfang* 厢房 (the hall on the left is the *dongxiang* 东厢 while the hall on the right is the *xixiang* 西厢).[5]

Construction and Structure

The abundance of timber in China makes it the most popular material used for the construction of low-rise buildings. Moreover with the high incidence of earthquakes in China it was found to be the most suitable material. To ensure that the structure of a building would withstand tremors of the earth the structural system of a building was designed to have flexible joints.[6] Thus, over the centuries the traditional construction method was developed, based on three basic systems, namely: the post and beam system; the column and tie beam system; and the log cabin system. The most commonly used is that of the post and beam which is also called the beam-frame system.

The traditional Chinese structural framework, built on a solid masonry podium, consists of rectangular bays of structural posts tied by longitudinal beams.[7] The beams and posts support a series of beams that rise toward the ridge in diminishing lengths. The struts support the rafters, the tiling boarding and the battens of the roof.[8] This system of construction is flexible and practical because by adjusting the levels of the longitudinal beams or purlins the profile and pitch of the roof can be determined.[9] Verandas can easily be added and large eaves and verge overhangs can be achieved by the use of brackets or *dougong* 斗拱. The lowest brackets are supported by systematically rising tiers and extend outward to support the large overhanging eaves and verge. The Chinese manual, *Yingzao Fashi*, published in 1103 AD records the *dougong* or bracketing system and its units of measurement. Basically there are four standard measurements, namely *fen* 分 (about 1 centimetre), *cai* 材 (fifteen *fen*), *qi* 契 (six *fen*) and *tiao* 挑 (about thirty *fen*).[10]

The proportion of every part of the *dougong* is measured in multiples of *fen*. The diameter of the column that supports the *dougong* varies from the column base. The *dougong* spread out in four directions carrying smaller brackets that may support others which spread out, thus, the whole bracketing system can be from one *cai* plus one *qi*, to three *cai*.[11]

The functions of the *dougong* or brackets are twofold: to give support to the large overhangs of verge and eaves giving ample sun shading and weather protection to the building, and to integrate the structural elements such as the beam-frame and

Changes in the beam-frame and brackets from the Tang to the Qing Dynasty according to Liang Shicheng

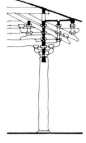

Fo Guangsi, Shanxi
Tang dynasty

Du Lesi, Guan Yinge, Hebei
Liao dynasty

Yong Shousi, Yu Huagong,
Shanxi
Song dynasty

Shan Fasi, Shanxi
Jin dynasty

Yang Helou, Hebei
Yuan dynasty

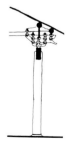

Zhi Fasi, Beijing
Ming dynasty

Wen Yuange, Beijing
Qing dynasty

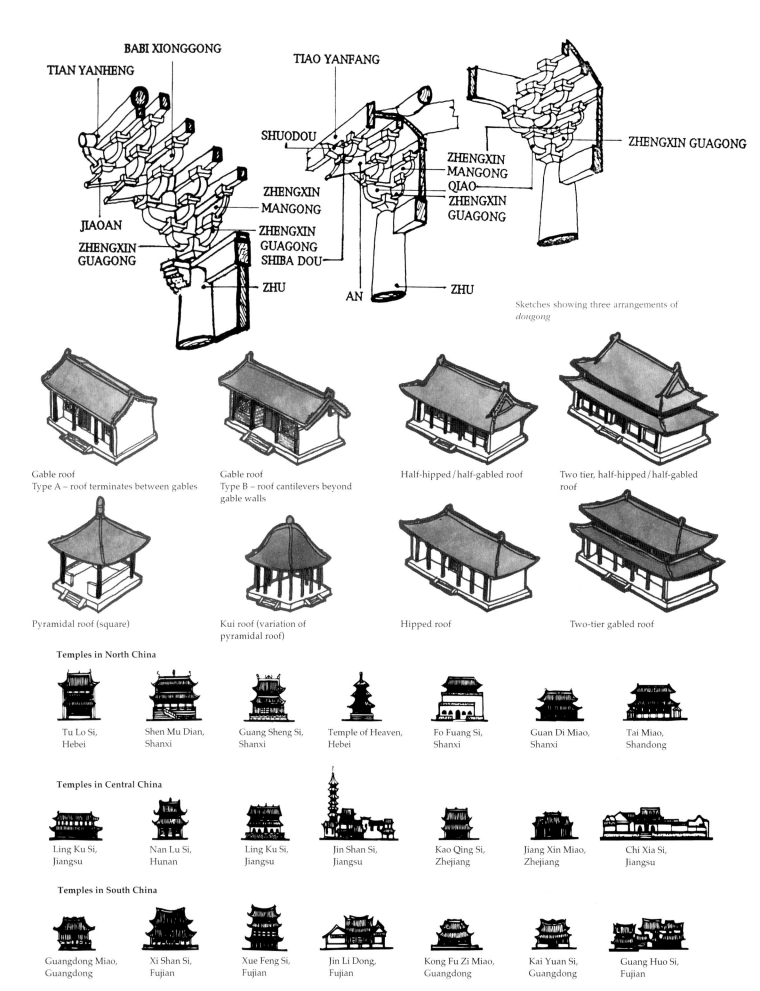

TIAN YANHENG

BABI XIONGGONG

JIAOAN

ZHENGXIN
GUAGONG

TIAO YANFANG

SHUODOU

ZHENGXIN
MANGONG

ZHENGXIN
GUAGONG
SHIBA DOU

ZHU

AN

ZHU

ZHENGXIN
MANGONG
QIAO
ZHENGXIN
GUAGONG

ZHENGXIN GUAGONG

Sketches showing three arrangements of *dougong*

Gable roof
Type A – roof terminates between gables

Gable roof
Type B – roof cantilevers beyond gable walls

Half-hipped / half-gabled roof

Two tier, half-hipped / half-gabled roof

Pyramidal roof (square)

Kui roof (variation of pyramidal roof)

Hipped roof

Two-tier gabled roof

Temples in North China

Tu Lo Si,
Hebei

Shen Mu Dian,
Shanxi

Guang Sheng Si,
Shanxi

Temple of Heaven,
Hebei

Fo Fuang Si,
Shanxi

Guan Di Miao,
Shanxi

Tai Miao,
Shandong

Temples in Central China

Ling Ku Si,
Jiangsu

Nan Lu Si,
Hunan

Ling Ku Si,
Jiangsu

Jin Shan Si,
Jiangsu

Kao Qing Si,
Zhejiang

Jiang Xin Miao,
Zhejiang

Chi Xia Si,
Jiangsu

Temples in South China

Guangdong Miao,
Guangdong

Xi Shan Si,
Fujian

Xue Feng Si,
Fujian

Jin Li Dong,
Fujian

Kong Fu Zi Miao,
Guangdong

Kai Yuan Si,
Guangdong

Guang Huo Si,
Fujian

Comparison of roof forms of temples in China

columns with decorative elements, for example the eaves finishes and the coffered ceiling finishes.[12]

There are many types of beam or *liang* in the beam-frame system but basically they can be classified according to section, depending on the number of *heng* 桁 or rafters. For example, in the section of the Tai Hedian the *san jialiang* 三架梁, the *wu jialiang* 五架梁, the *qi jialiang* 七架梁 are used to support the rafters (the *shang jinheng* 上金桁, the *zhong jinheng* 中金桁, the *xia jinheng* 下金桁) and the roofing materials. In a pyramidal roof the *liang* are named *shunliang* 顺梁 and *baliang* 扒梁. Many types of columns are used; the commonest are *zhizhu* 直拄 and *suozhu* 梭柱.

Bracketing System

The *dougong* (timber brackets) are constructed to give support to the large cantilevered verge and eaves overhangs. They consist of many interlocking parts of timber to form a bracket.[13] There are many types of *dougong*. Two basic types are called *neiyan* 内檐 and *waiyan* 外檐. The *waiyan* is subdivided into *shangyan* 上檐 and *xiayan* 下檐. Those placed at the top of the internal columns are called *zhutou kedougong* 挂头科斗拱 which again can be divided into various types such as *dadou* 大斗 and *shibadou* 十八斗.[14] Those under the eaves and verge are named *pingshen kedougong* 平身科斗拱.[15] Those supporting the corner of a building roof are called *jiaoke dougong* 角科斗拱. Each bracket consists of various types of *dougong*, each having a particular name such as *zhenxin guagong* 正心瓜拱, or *xianggong* 厢拱.

Roof Form

Generally there are four types of traditional roof: the gabled, the hipped, the half-hipped/half-gabled and the pyramidal. These four roof forms may vary to form two or three tier roofs with the combination of two or more basic roof forms. The most important building is usually covered by a multi-tiered, hipped roof which is used mainly for religious or imperial palatial structures. The half-hipped/half-gabled roof is also used for important buildings.[16] The more important the building the more tiers of roof it has. The other less commonly used roof forms are: lean-to roof, flat roof, *lu* and *shizhiji* 十字脊 roof.

The basic roof forms were created during the Han dynasty. By the Qing dynasty these were developed to create many variations of roof. The pyramidal was built in various forms of geometry such as round, square, pentagonal, hexagonal and octagonal. Round roofs were used for religious buildings, square for pavilions and octagonal for pagodas.

In China there are mainly three types of ridge and roof corner design. In north China the most significant type has a straight roof ridge and the gable end corner ribs tilt slightly upwards. In central China the roof ridge is straight but the gable end roof corner ribs tilt up. But in south China the roof ridge is curved and the roof corner ribs tilt and curve upwards.[17] The exaggerated upturn of the corners of the eaves, according to many scholars, was due to the aesthetic refinement of the elevational treatment of a building.[18]

Roof Section

A Chinese roof section is decided by the designer or builder but it is based on specific rules as set out by the master builders of traditional buildings. The pitch of the main ridge of a traditional building in most parts of China is still built modelled on the proportioning system as spelt out in the *Yingzao Fashi*. It is influenced by the positioning of the structural columns and the beam-frame system of the roof making

Various plan forms for pavilions:

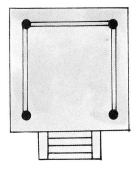

SQUARE PLAN (usually covered by a pyramidal roof). Four columns support a series of beams which in turn support the *leigong zhu* (vertical struts) under the rafters.

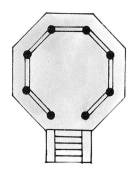

OCTAGONAL PLAN (usually covered by a pyramidal roof). This arrangement requires greater skills of joinery but follows the same structural principles as above.

ROUND PLAN (usually covered by a pyramidal roof). Depending on the diameter of the plan between four to eight or more columns are used to construct this style of pavilion.

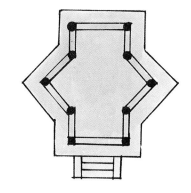

PLANS DERIVED FROM GEOMETRY These include various other plans such as the triangular, five-sided, six-sided, and plans intersecting two squares or two circles.

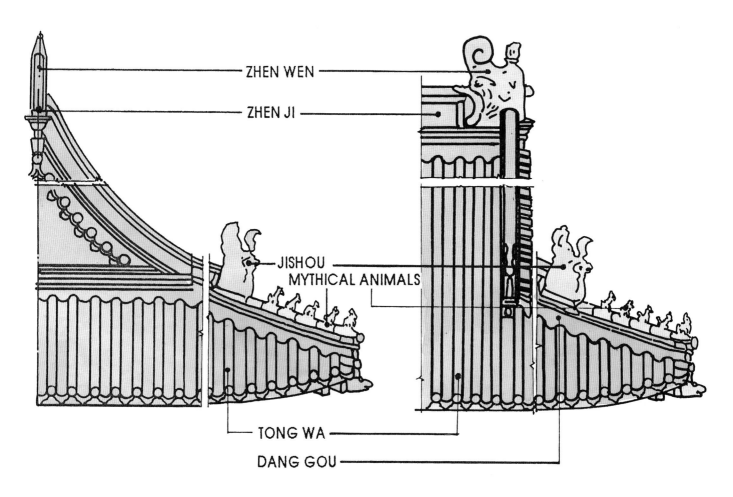

ZHEN WEN

ZHEN JI

JISHOU
MYTHICAL ANIMALS

TONG WA

DANG GOU

Roof detail of tile layout, *zhenwen* and mythical
animals on hipped roof (left) and half-hipped/
half-gabled roof.

Various shapes and names of tiles

Banwa, used as under-layer tiles

Zhiyao banwa, used as under-layer tiles
near the ridge

Dishui, used as edge tiles

Tian goutou, used for channelling water

Zhusi tongwa, bamboo tiles

Goutou used as edge tiles

the Chinese roof profile most flexible.[19] By adjusting the column height and position the pitch and profile of the roof can be changed.

Roof sections can be classified by the number of *bujia* 步架 (the vertical strut or post that support the horizontal members). When a roof has five *bujia* it is classified as a *wujia* roof. If it has six *jia* then it is called a *liujia* roof. The *jujia* 举架 or tilt of the rafters is also an influential factor that determines the pitch of the roof.

Roof Decorations

Roof decoration and design are not confined to the sculptural elements displayed on the roof ridges and corners. The roof form, tile design and ornaments are all integral. Most traditional Chinese buildings have roof ornaments on the roof ridges or corner ribs.[20] These ornaments range from dancing dragons to figurines. For religious buildings the dancing dragons symbolising active *yang* forces are flanked by the pearl which is a *yin* element. The chimera, the lion, the horse and the unicorn represent *yang* while the phoenix and floral sculptures symbolise *yin*. Sometimes figurines such as the gods of thunder and rain are placed on the corner ribs as symbols of natural forces. Generally the roof is covered by bamboo tiles finished by edge tiles that allow rain water to fall down like a *zhulian* 珠廉 (string of pearls). The roof ridge is terminated with *wenshou* 吻兽 and the corner ribs decorated with glazed ceramic figures ranging from figurines to dragons.

Roof Tiles

There are basically two types of tiles, namely *xiao* 小 and *tongban*. The *xiao* are flat and also called butterfly tiles, suitable for use to cover all types of roof; whereas the *tongban* are cylindrical and used for prestigious buildings. The *tongban* may be made from clay or glazed. The colours of tiles range from yellow to grey. Prior to and during the Qing dynasty yellow was used exclusively for the royal families.

Tiles used during the Ming and Qing dynasties varied from flat to curved in order to give the perfect finish to the roof. Each shape has a particular name.

Colour Scheme

Colour schemes for buildings were developed from the Chunqiu era to the Ming dynasty. Bright colours were popular during the early periods.[21]

Traditional Chinese buildings are not designed with the sole consideration of building form but also with respect to the symbolism of colours. The application of paint on timber serves the purpose of protecting the timber and gives symbolic significance to the building elements. The use of colours in Chinese building is a unique art and an understanding of the significance of Chinese colours must therefore be grasped before specific colours are applied.

Chinese colours can be made from various materials such as minerals and plants. There are rules and principles with regard to colour schemes applied on the building and its components. These rules were written down in architectural records such as the *Yingzao Fashi*. Colours are not applied merely to building structures: they are also applied to building elements such as columns, beams, struts, roof tiles and even decorative motifs.

Each colour relates to one of the Five Elements and has its own significance and symbolic value for the Chinese. Green, related to the Wood Element, symbolises growth and is used to represent longevity and, because of its soothing effect, also to represent harmony. Red, a bright, auspicious colour associated with warmth and the Fire Element, represents good fortune and happiness.

Zhenwen, used to terminate the main ridge

Xianren, used to terminate the rib corner of a roof

Cun jishou, used as roof ornament and placed next to the *xianren* ornament

Example of *xianren* (from the Zhuangluncang in the Yi Heyuan)

Column bases

Round base

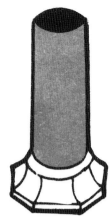

Octagonal base

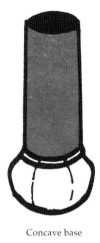

Concave base

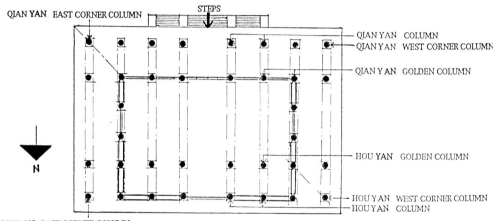

Plan showing types of column

QIAN YAN EAST CORNER COLUMN

STEPS

QIAN YAN COLUMN
QIAN YAN WEST CORNER COLUMN

QIAN YAN GOLDEN COLUMN

HOU YAN GOLDEN COLUMN

HOU YAN WEST CORNER COLUMN
HOU YAN COLUMN

HOU YAN EAST CORNER COLUMN

N

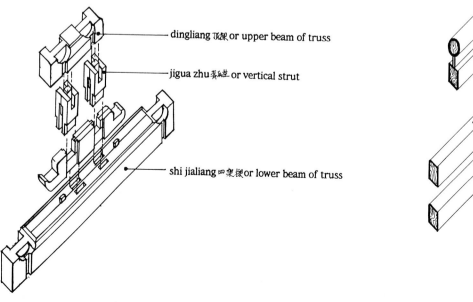

dingliang 頂樑 or upper beam of truss

jigua zhu 脊瓜柱 or vertical strut

shi jialiang 四架樑 or lower beam of truss

Joinery of the truss of the beam-framed structure

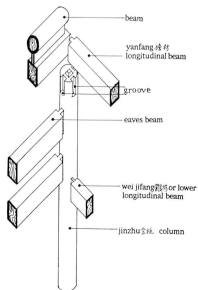

beam

yanfang 簷枋 longitudinal beam

groove

eaves beam

wei jifang 圍脊枋 or lower longitudinal beam

jinzhu 金柱 column

Joinery of the column, cross and longitudinal beams

Yellow, the royal colour used by the emperors, symbolises power and authority. It also has associations with the Earth Element which symbolises growth. Black, linked to the Water Element, denotes darkness. White is for mourning and is associated with the Gold Element.[22]

Walls

Walls are non-structural because the structural supports for the roofs and floors are columns, beams, beam-frames, and brackets. Walls are built as enclosures and screens. In the event of an earthquake, the walls may collapse but the light timber structural frame of post and beam is more flexible and more likely to withstand the earth's movement than heavy masonry walls.[23] Secondly the walls, being non-structural, may be built thicker or thinner according to the climatic conditions rather than to structural requirements. Materials used depend on the purpose the wall serves.

For example, in the north where the climate is more severe than the south, the walls may be much thicker. In other cases walls may not be required at all. Some masonry walls are built to contain the roof ends like party walls and fire partitions. Masonry walls may be built of bricks, stones or mud.

Various names have been given to the walls of a building. The central end gable-wall is called *shanqiang* 山墙, the end portion of the end wall is named *langqiang* 廊墙, the front facade wall is *qian yanqiang* 前檐墙, the rear facade wall is *hou yanqiang* 后檐墙 and the internal partition wall is *ge duanqiang* 隔断墙. Walls are classified according to their shapes. For example, an angular gable wall is an Earth Element.[24] Various names are also given to types of walls depending on the ways in which they are used and the purposes they serve.

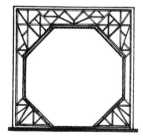

The timber used for traditional classical buildings such as the palaces in the Forbidden City is of the best quality (eg *nanmu* 楠木 and *hua limu* 花梨木) even when the wall is used for screen or infill and is non-structural. Details of the infill walls and windows of the palaces of the Gugong are intricate and of excellent workmanship.[25]

Columns

Columns in a traditional Chinese building are placed in a regular rhythm. Each column is given a name depending on its position.[26]

Columns are very important structural elements and are constructed of hardwood. As mentioned earlier there are many types of column although some sources state that there are basically two types, the *zhi* and the *suo*. The former is straight while the latter has a smaller diameter at the top and bottom and a larger diameter at the middle of the column. During the Qing dynasty five types of column commonly used are the *yanzhu* 檐柱, the *jinzhu* 金柱 , *chongyan jinzhu* 重檐金柱, *tongzhu* 童柱, and the *zhongzhu* 中柱.

The section of the columns may be square, round or polygonal (from five to eight sides), rectangular or composite in section. They should be well-seasoned before they are used for construction as insufficient seasoning may cause them to split.[27]

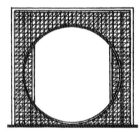

The proportional ratio of the height and the cross-sectional dimension of the column is designed to give the column a good sense of proportion. During the Tang the proportional ratio of height to width was 8:1 to 9:1. By the Song dynasty it was 11:1 to 14:1 as the column became more slender. During the Ming and Qing dynasties it was 9:1 to 11:1.[28]

The main columns in important buildings are usually decorated with gilded patterns of *yin* and *yang* symbols. Some granite columns are elaborately carved with entwined

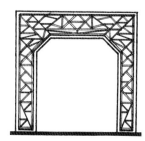

Window grilles or latticework can be made in timber, glazed pottery, granite, glazed bamboo pieces, stone or marble. The decorative patterns of the lattice give symbolic significance to the window.

Zhenta kejai (slanting pattern)

Panchang (elongated pattern)

Guaizijin (variable pattern)

Pingleiwen (broken ice pattern)

Guibeijin (tortoiseshell pattern)

Window shapes:

Peach-shaped

Square

Round

Five-sided

Double-square shaped

Fan-shaped

Octagonal

Door elevations

dragons. Stone bases are usually used to raise the columns off the ground for damp-proofing and to prevent the columns from being damaged.[29] The shapes of column bases range from round to octagonal and follow the shapes of the column. The detailing of the column's connection with the base varies depending on the shape of the column. For example, if the column is round the top of the base is cut round to fit the column.

Windows, Doors and Openings

The windows of a traditional building are not just used to exclude the weather but are also decorative elements. Very often the window frames are made to house intricate carved panels that portray legends and symbols expressed by the exquisite art of wood carving and latticework. The variety and size of windows are numerous. Windows are made of hardwood and are often side or top hinged. Each part of the window has a particular name.

A window consists of three parts, namely the *chuang* 窗 or opening, the *chuang kuang* 窗框 or window frame, and the *chuang ling* 窗棂 or latticework. The shape of the opening may be square, round, geometric in form or even modelled on the shape of an animal or an object.[30] The latticework is rich in the variety of patterns ranging from geometric to abstract forms.[31]

Doors are also mainly made of wood with frames and infills of latticework or panels. The patterns of the latticework range from blossoms to geometric patterns. The detailing of a door is carefully worked out in terms of joinery and decorative motif.[32] Some of the doors built for the imperial palaces in the Gugong are studded with *mending* 门钉 (metal bosses).[33] The bosses are gilded and detailed to protrude. Metal mounts called *menhuan* 门环 are often installed on doors.[34]

Main doors are not complete without decorative elements placed in front of them. The most common elements are the stone or granite lions or the stone drums. The stone lions are displayed in pairs. The male on the left plays with a ball while the female on the right holds a cub. The former has its mouth open and the latter its mouth closed. The stone drum can be carved with spirals, floral motifs and inset with mirrors. Very often spaces are divided by partition doors that are folding or sliding. The colour scheme of doors is either very bright or left as natural timber. Joinery of doors and windows is usually done by skilled artisans.

Openings in walls are in many forms and shapes ranging from oval to triangular. Each shape is of symbolic significance, and on a single garden wall there may be a variety of shapes and sizes. The openings frame the views beyond and open up particular vistas.

Ceilings

Chinese ceilings of important buildings are highly decorative. Basically there are two types of ceiling. The first type is called *tianhua* 天花 and is a false ceiling created by battens with finishing battens or boardings. The second is called *zaojing* 藻井 or caisson and it is applied on a coffered ceiling of a palace to give significant symbolism and meaning to the interior space.[35] The caissons are usually constructed in several tiers which range from square to circular.[36]

Square caissons on coffered ceilings are constructed by intersecting laths at 90 degrees. The panels set in between the laths are painted with significant colours – the colours symbolic of the wishes of the inhabitants. Red means happiness, green longevity, blue heavenly blessing, yellow imperial power and gold royalty.

A variation of the caisson-coffered ceiling is the *juanpeng* 卷棚. This is unique

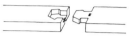

Joinery details of the columns and beams

Joinery details of the timber pieces

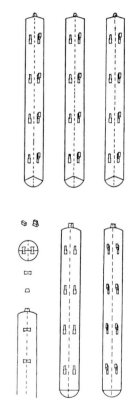

Joinery of column sections

Types of balustrade:

Baluster capped with animal
sitting on a lotus

Baluster with carved capital

Baluster capped with lotus motif

Brick and stone paving:

Screen partition with *guibeijin* latticework

Screen partition with *pingleiwen* latticework

because the central portion consists of brackets spiralling like a whirlwind towards the centre of the ceiling.

Another method used to construct the ornamental ceiling involved a mixture of bamboo, hemp cloth, paper and wood. This method is used for building ceilings of less important buildings. Patterns and decorative motifs range from leaf scrolls to fruits and flowers. Each theme has particular significance. For example, pomegranates symbolise posterity, peonies beauty, lotuses uprightness, scrollwork scholarship, phoenix *yin* qualities and power, crane longevity, and dragon *yang* power. The shape of the ceiling also signifies its symbolism, for example the circular ceiling relates to the heavens and the square the earth.

Podiums and Balustrades

A Chinese building is built on a raised podium which is integral to the overall design of the building.[37] The more important the building the higher the podium.[38] Its purpose can be twofold: firstly, to waterproof against rising damp since most Chinese buildings are built of timber; and secondly, for aesthetic reasons: a podium gives a sense of importance to the building and its height must correspond to the rest of the building elements.[39] Masonry is used for podiums, which usually follow the shape of the building.[40] The foundation and podium of a Chinese building are modelled on the traditional way of building.[41] The various parts of the podium are given particular names. The height of the podium should be proportional to the height of the columns and is governed by the number of steps. The podiums for the imperial palaces of the Ming and Qing dynasties were raised at least nine steps high. Buildings for officials were raised three or five steps. The imperial rulers were carried through the buildings over the Yulushi 御路石 which were carved with dragons and clouds.

When a podium is sufficiently high as to require balustrades the design has to be executed with care so that they are in harmony and complement each other. The balustrades should be designed to enhance not just the podium but also the entire building. Its proportion and detailing have to be worked out with reference to the overall design and the type and usage of building.[42]

Many stone balustrades in the Gugong are intricately carved and magnificently built. Care was taken to demonstrate the rank of the building by creating various cappings for the posts of balustrades. In the Gugong dragon and phoenix motifs were used for the most important imperial palaces, whereas lotus and other floral themes were used for the balustrades of less important buildings.

A balustrade consists of upstands or posts and infill panels or balusters. The upstands rest on the *difu* 地栿, a stone piece with grooves to house the upstands and balusters. The upstands are usually capped with carved ornaments such as upturned lotus buds or mythical animals or other auspicious objects. Sometimes the corner upstands of a balustrade are detailed in such a way that they are incorporated with water spouts that are carved as ornamental elements such as dragon or lion heads.

Paving Slabs and Bricks

Stones and bricks are used to pave the indoor and outdoor floors of a traditional Chinese building.[43] The skill of polishing the paving slabs was developed as early as the Han dynasty and further developed during the Tang and Song dynasties.[44] During the Qing dynasty marble and *jinzhuan* 金砖 or large, well-fired paving slabs were used for floors and the paths of the spirits. Also known as 'spirit ways' these are the central paths through the imperial palaces and temples over which the emperor would be carried in his sedan chair.

Various motifs and decorative patterns:

Floral patterns found on the stone entrance of a Han dynasty tomb

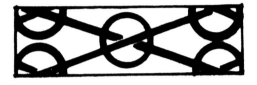

Geometric patterns found on the stone entrance of a Han dynasty tomb

Pattern derived from natural phenomena (thunder) found on a stele in Luoyang dated Han dynasty

Pattern derived from natural phenomena (waves) found on a stele of a Han tomb

Pattern derived from mythical animal (dragon) found on a stone stele of a tomb in Sichuan

The sizes and shapes of paving slabs, the types of materials and the paving patterns vary depending on the type and rank of buildings.[45] However, the patterns are intended to communicate auspicious significance. For example, the *shi zhifeng* 十字缝 (a pattern based on the word *shi* 十 or ten) and the *guai* or *ren* 人 (pattern depicting posterity) are commonly used.

For landscape gardens, stone pebbles and granite slabs are also used side by side with bricks. The variety of paving patterns is complex and interesting. Some, for example, are based on floral and geometric patterns and most are rich not just in variety but also in texture and colour.

Decorative Motifs

Basically there are seven types of decorative motifs for application on structural and non-structural elements which are:

- modelled on animals such as the dragon, phoenix, tortoise and unicorn;
- derived from plants and trees such as the peony, chrysanthemum, orchid, pine or bamboo;
- derived from natural forces such as lightning, rain or wind;
- stylised from human or supernatural figures such as the Immortals or Taoist deities;
- originating from geometric motifs such as circles, squares or rectangles;
- derived from auspicious Chinese words such as *kou* 口, *ding* 丁 or *shou* 寿;
- derived from precious utensils or objects such as bronze tripods, coins or pearls.

Decorative and utility objects such as lanterns, brush paintings and wall murals are also used which relate Chinese legends and values. For example, the Immortals holding peaches standing under pine trees beside some deer signify auspicious and good tidings of longevity. The Immortals, the pine trees and peaches represent longevity, and the deer luck and heavenly blessings. The throne of Qing emperor Guang Xu was engraved intricately with a scenic landscape. The pavilions and corridors of the Changlang 长廊 of the Yi Heyuan 颐和园 are decorated with hundreds of exquisite paintings.[46]

The roof termination of a round building can be decorated in many ways. For example, the Qian Qiuting 千秋亭 in the Gugong has an umbrella-like structure capped by a pearl and supported by a vase-like structure flanked by snake/dragon-like motifs. Generally the tops of round buildings are capped by the *baoding* 宝顶 which can be designed in various forms.

As mentioned earlier, roofs are ornamented and terminated by *wenshou* 吻兽, *chuishou* 垂兽 or *jiaoshou* 角兽.[47] The edge tiles are moulded with patterns derived from auspicious words such as *fu* 福, *shou* 寿, or *lu* 禄; or they may be derived from plants that portray beauty or longevity. The sizes and dimensions of these ornaments are spelt out in the *Yingzao Fashi*.

The structural beams of a traditional building are often transformed into sculptural elements derived from auspicious symbols such as lotus buds or from popular legends of heroes and immortals. Structural timber brackets are carved so intricately that they appear purely decorative.[48]

Main doors are very important elements. Built with hardwood, they are often beautifully carved with symbols such as deer, bats and floral themes that portray good fortune. Doors for imperial households are carved with dragon images, and main doors are decorated with *mending*. Internal doors have infills of timber lattice-work. Paintings of the door gods are often executed on doors of religious buildings.

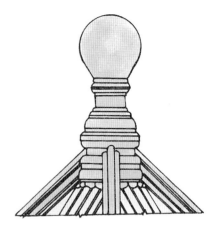

Decorative motifs are not confined to three-dimensional forms: wall murals are also used as motifs. Paintings of beautiful landscapes, fairies and deities are often seen on the walls of important buildings. Very often calligraphic inscriptions and words are painted or engraved on pottery panels and placed above doors or windows as decorative elements.

Furniture is not only for utility but rather is treated decoratively. A piece of furniture is beautifully shaped and finished with decorative motifs that are in harmony with the rest of the interior.[49] The symbols used depend on the status of the owners.

The decorative motifs for coffered ceilings, doors, windows, balustrades and screens are endlessly rich in variety and form. Their colour schemes are equally rich in hue and tonal value. A Chinese building is not only to be experienced and understood by moving through its spaces and studying its structures but also to be appreciated by understanding the symbolism of its decorative motifs.

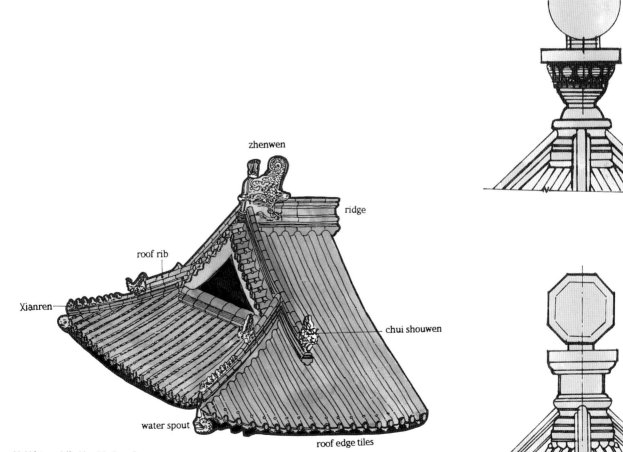

Half-hipped/half-gabled roof

Notes

1 See Liu Qijun 刘奇俊, *Zhongguo Gujian Zhu* 中国古建筑, Yishu Jia Chuban She 艺术家出版社 (Taibei), 1987, p13.

2 See *Zhou Li* 周礼 also known as *Zhouguanjing* 周官经, one of the Confucian Classics written by Zhougong 周公. It states that before the setting up of a capital or palace the orientation and *feng shui* must be assessed. See also the section on *kanyu* in Chapter 7 pp60-75.

3 The largest building may have five or more courtyards. See Wang Yunwu pp 45-47. The variable of *si heyuan* may be found in size, scale and proportion but the fundamental principle of enclosing the four sides of a square or rectangular courtyard with building blocks does not vary.

4 Refer to drawings on p27 for the various plan forms which are commonly used for building pavilions.

5 The *mingtang* faces south and is a Fire Element, the east hall is Wood Element, the west Gold Element and the north Water Element.

6 In 1975 and 1976 major earthquakes occurred in Tang Shan 唐山 and Liaoning Haicheng 辽宁海城 respectively. The major timber buildings such as Du Lesi 独乐寺, Guan Yinge 观音阁 were not damaged.

7 The Chinese name each bay of a building *jian* 间. The central bay is named *mingjian* 明间 while the side *cijian* 次间. The number of bays should be an odd (*yang*) number, either 3, 5, 7, 9 or 11. For example, the Tai Hedian is made up of eleven bays to demonstrate its *yang*. In the Qing and Ming dynasties the number of bays of the residential homes of government officials was governed by the rank of the officials. Those of low rank could only build houses of three bays.

8 This type of construction was recorded on the caves of Han dynasty tombs. See Ren Jiyu 任继愈 (ed), *Zhongguo Wenhua Shizhi Congshu* 中国文化史知识丛书, Zhongguo Gudai Jianzhu 中国古代建筑, Zhongguo Zhongyang Dangxiao Chuban She 中国中央党校出版社, 1991, p2.

9 The flexibility allows movement and helps to withstand earthquakes.

10 A special ruler called Lubanche 鲁班尺 was used for the measurement. One foot of the Lubanche was 32 centimetres.

11 See Li Jie 李诚, *Yingzao Fashi* 营造法式, AD 1103.

12 The high point of development was during the Song dynasty.

13 The joints of the brackets allow certain flexibility and movement which enables the structure to survive earth tremors.

14 See drawing on p26 for the various types of *dougong* and figure on p25 for the changes of the beam-frame systems and brackets from the Tang to the Qing dynasty according to Liang Shicheng. Note the changes in the ratio of column heights and *dougong* sizes.

15 The eaves can be cantilevered and supported in four ways: the *chuan* 椽 (rafters) cantilevered; the brackets cantilevered; masonry supports cantilevered; and the *tiao* built up with *dougong* to support the *yan* 檐 (eaves).

16 Buildings with hipped roofs or half-hipped/half-gabled roofs are usually built with an odd number of bays to increase the power of *yang* because they are important buildings.

17 Buildings built before the Ming dynasty were usually constructed with tilted-up roof corners. See Wenfa Bu Wenwu Baohu Kejiushuo 文化部文物保护科究所, *Zhongguo Gudai Jianzhu Xiushan Jishu* 中国古代建筑修缮技术, Zhongguo Jianzhu Gongyi Chuban She 中国建筑工业出版社 (Beijing) 1983, p89.

18 See Wang Yunwu, op cit, and also see Boyd, Andrew, op cit, p39. Also refer to Lip, Evelyn, *Chinese Temple Architecture in Singapore*, PhD Thesis, National University of Singapore (Singapore) 1984, p37.

19 See illustration on p30 for the names of columns in a plan.

20 The roof ridge was first created to add weight to the roof so that it would not be blown off during a storm. The various parts of a roof are as follows: the main ridge is *zhengwen* 正吻, the corner ribs are *qiangji* 钱脊, and corner ribs of the lower tiers of roof are *jiaoji* 角脊.

21 See Liu Dunzhen 刘敦帧, *Zhongguo Gudai Jianzhu Shi* 中国古代建筑史 Zhongguo Jianzhu Gongye Chuban She 中国建筑工业出版社 (Beijing) 1980, p17.

22 See Lip, Evelyn, *Chinese Geomancy*, Times Books International (Singapore) 1979, p13. The use of bright colours for buildings was noted in ancient writings such as the *Zuo Zhuan* 左传, dated third century.

23 See Ren Jiyu (ed), op cit, p3. Some buildings were known to have withstood a few earthquakes and yet its timber structural components remained intact. Also see Zhongguo Jianzhu Shi Pian Xiezhu 中国建筑史编写组, *Zhongguo Jianzhu Shi* 中国建筑史, Zhongguo Jianzhu Gongyi Chuban She 中国建筑工业出版社 (Beijing) 1982, p152.

24 See figures on p24 for the various types and elements of wall.

25 Both during the Ming dynasty and before, the craftsmen with special skills in China were not allowed to change their profession and they were supposed to hand down their art of craftsmanship to future generations so that their knowledge would not be lost. Many craftsmen were retained to work in the palaces and their male children were trained to carry on with their forefathers' crafts.

26 See *Zhongguo Jianzhu Shi*, op cit, p190.

27 Metal rings are used to hold split columns.

28 See Lin Huicheng 林会承, *Chuantong Jianzhu Shouce* 传统建筑手册, Yishu Jiachu Banshe Yinhang 艺术家出版社印行 (Taipei) 1989, p83.

29 Bronze bases were used during the Shang dynasty. By the time of the Han dynasty stone bases were very common.

30 The round window is called *yuedong* 月洞 and the octagonal is *baguachuang* 八卦窗.

31 The variety includes square, crosses, tortoise shells and bamboo grilles. Sometimes calligraphic words such as *kou* 口 and *ya* 亚 are stylised and used as patterns.

32 Chinese joinery is famous for its intricate detailing where no nails are used to join timber members together.

33 Originally, *mending* were created to cover the joints but later became prestigious elements.

34 During the Qing dynasty the materials used for making the *menhuan* indicated the rank and position of the owner in society. For the emperor's palaces the *menhuan* was gilded. For his relatives it was bronze and for officials steel. See Lin Huicheng, ibid, p107.

35 During the Song period caissons were named *qijing* 绮井. By the Qing dynasty the design of the coffered ceiling had developed in such a way that the central portion of an imperial ceiling was often painted with dragons and was called *longjing*. There was a rule for determining the height of a ceiling for an imperial palace or temple. The height must be of a supreme *yang* measurement (eg the ceiling of the Qi Niandian is 9 yards and 9 feet high). The traditional colour schemes of ceilings were created during the Warring States era.

36 During the Qing dynasty the caissons were usually built in three tiers.

37 Podiums were built as early as the Warring States period. See *Yu Zhuoyun*, op cit, p212.

38 Important buildings may have a two-tiered podium. The higher podium is called *taiji* 台基. The Qi Niandian sits on a three-tiered podium.

39 The builders during the Song to Qing dynasty regarded the design of the podium as of vital importance. *Yingzao Fashi* and *Gongcheng Zuofa Zelie* 工程做法则例 contain the rules of thumb for building a podium.

40 The podium is circular for the Temple of Heaven, rectangular for the Tai Hedian and square for the Zhong Hedian. For religious buildings the podium that supports the balustrades is named *xu mizuo* 须弥座.

41 See three-dimensional drawing on p24 for illustration.

42 The podium and balustrades of religious buildings are designed differently from residential buildings. The symbols used for a religious building are related to the religious symbols and beliefs.

43 As early as the Warring States and Qin eras brick tiles were already made in various shapes in intricately designed patterns.

44 See *Yingzao Fashi*, op cit, chapter 15. See the illustrations on p34 for some examples of paving patterns of bricks and stones.

45 The names of bricks are often related to their sizes. For example, the two feet square slab is called *er chizhuan*.

46 Refer to p95 for paintings in the Changlang. The columns are painted red and the longitudinal and cross beams are painted with vivid patterns.

47 Most of the roof ornaments are derived from living creatures or plants and are symbols that are related to water or water supply.

48 See figures on pp24, 26 for illustrations.

49 See illustration on p95 for an example.

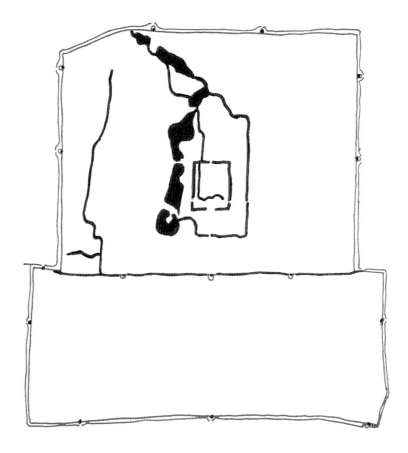

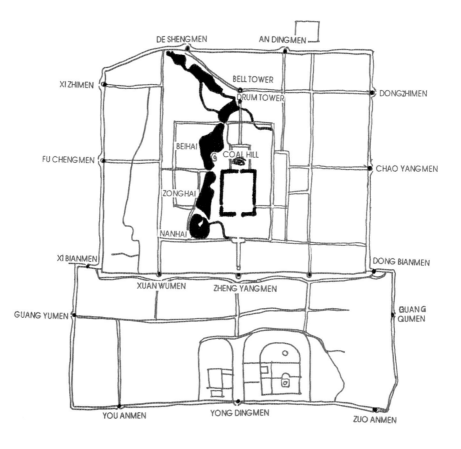

DE SHENGMEN

AN DINGMEN

XI ZHIMEN

BELL TOWER

DRUM TOWER

DONGZHIMEN

BEIHAI

COAL HILL

FU CHENGMEN

CHAO YANGMEN

ZONGHAI

NANHAI

XI BIANMEN

DONG BIANMEN

XUAN WUMEN

ZHENG YANGMEN

GUANG YUMEN

GUANG QUMEN

YOU ANMEN

YONG DINGMEN

ZUO ANMEN

Beijing

Beijing 北京 is the capital and political administrative centre of the People's Republic of China. Its population is about eleven million. Its numerous monuments, museums, ancient traditional structures, cultural palaces, libraries, art galleries, memorial halls, gymnasiums and religious buildings make it one of the world's most important and most attractive tourist centres. Its historical past is long and its cultural and architectural heritage are rich.[1]

Beijing was first inhabited half a million years ago and it first began to develop into a significant city during the Warring States era (403–221 BC);[2] a period in which the many states of China were divided by continuous conflict. Some of the prominent states were: Qi, Chu, Wu, Lu, Wei, Cai, Zheng, Cao, Chen Song and Yan. Beijing was the capital of Yan. It was destroyed when the warring lords were conquered by Qinshi Huangdi, but later rebuilt during the Han dynasty. During the Tang and the Wu Dai periods it was named Tai Yuan 太原 and it became the centre for commerce and arts. At the beginning of the Liao dynasty, Khitan Tartars constructed an impressive palace in the southwest of Tai Yuan which was destroyed by the Liao tribes in AD 947. However, the Liaos had left a notable monument to house the Buddhist Tripitaka in Beijing, the Tian Ningsi pagoda near the Guang Anmen.[3] Tai Yuan was rebuilt as Zhong Du 中都 by the Manchurians who established the Jin dynasty.[4] In AD 1153 during the reign of Zhen Yuan 贞元 it was renamed Beijing 北京 (Capital City in the North).

In AD 1263 Beijing was chosen by Kublai Khan as the political centre of China. He moved his capital from Karakorum to Beijing and called it Dadu 大都 (Capital City). Civil war started in AD 1399 under the leadership of Zhu Yuanzhang 朱元璋 and it ended when the Yuan era was over. China was controlled by Zhu Yuanzhang who formed the Ming dynasty. Dadu was not regarded as the capital but rather it was considered as a city signifying peace and so it was named Beiping 北平 (Peace in the North). However, under the rule of the third emperor of the Ming dynasty, Yong Le, Beiping was again made the capital in AD 1402 and much building and construction works were carried out. Because the topography of the city was flat it was laid out as a square with plots of land subdivided into a rectilinear pattern with the main roads being 25 metres wide.[5] The city walls were classified as *gongcheng* 宫城, *huangcheng* 皇城 and *ducheng* 都城. The former was built for the security of the imperial palaces while the latter for the city. The outer city boundary measured about 8,000 by 3,100 metres and the south had three gateways while the east and west had only one gateway. Indeed, Beijing was laid out like a chess board divided into distinct quarters. The central portion, containing the imperial administrative and residential palaces, was the heart from which other areas grew.[6]

The construction of the imperial palaces started with the Ming rulers. Emperor Cheng Zu 成祖 moved his capital from Nanjing to Beijing and built the Zi Jincheng in the centre of the city as his administrative centre and residential home. The importance of the imperial palace complex was marked by the four main gateways, namely Dong Huamen 东华门, Xi Huamen 夏华门, Wumen 午门 and Shen Wumen.

Plan of Zi Jincheng showing the water courses that enhance the *feng shui* of the natural environment.

Plan of the Zi Jincheng and Huayuan showing main gateways. The main access into the Forbidden City is through the Tiananmen.

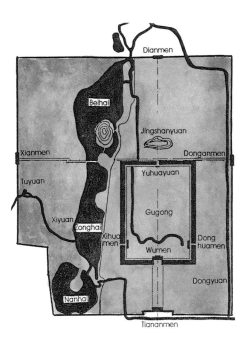

Plan of the Zi Jincheng and Huayuan

When the Qing rulers came into power rapid development of the city into a political centre started. About eight hundred palatial buildings, temples and monuments were constructed. Beijing remained basically divided into three sections: the outer city, the inner Huangcheng 皇城 (imperial city) and the Zi Jincheng 紫禁城 (Forbidden City). The Zi Jincheng was slightly north of the centre of Beijing. The road system divides the city into rectilinear blocks of buildings ventilated by courtyards.

When the Nationalist revolution succeeded, Beijing was given up as the capital and its name reverted back to Beiping. It fell into the hands of the Japanese invaders in 1937. In AD 1949, however, the Communists took control and Mao Zedong proclaimed Beijing the capital of the People's Republic of China. Since then 150,000 square metres of new buildings have been built.

Beijing can now be divided into two areas – the inner city and the outer city. The inner city contains the Huangcheng (the imperial palaces) and its most impressive open square named Tiananmen 天安门 (the Gate of Heavenly Peace). This square, measuring 500 metres from east to west and 880 metres from north to south, is the grand approach to the Zi Jincheng, to the east of which are some historical mosques. On the north are the Coal Hill and the Museum of Fine Arts. Further north are the Drum and Bell Towers built by Qing emperor, Yong Le in AD 1420. The Drum Tower was constructed with materials taken from the ancient tower dating back to the Yuan dynasty. The Bell Tower was built later in AD 1745.

To the northwest and west are the Beihai, the Zhonghai and the Nanhai. During the Liao dynasty (in AD 907) the emperor used to have his *ligong* 离宫 (resort palace) on the Beihai Park. Further west are situated the National Library, the Luxun Museum and prominent temples such as the Bai Tasi 白塔寺 built in the Liao era. The Luxun Museum was formerly the residence of China's well-known author, Luxun 鲁迅, who wrote a number of striking novels which reflect the society of his era.

In the outskirts of northwest Beijing are situated many landscaped gardens. In AD 1703, during the reign of emperor Kang Xi, some of the gardens built were: the Jin Mingyuan 静明园, the Chang Chunyuan 畅春园, the Xi Huayuan 西花园, the Han Fangyuan 含芳园, the Ji Xianyuan 集贤园, the Xi Chunyuan 熙春园, the Zhi Yiyuan 自怡园 and the Yuan Mingyuan 园明园. By AD 1750, during the reign of Qian Long, many more gardens were built: the Qing Yiyuan 清漪园, the Chang Chunyuan 畅春园, the Wan Chunyuan 万春园, the Shu Chunyuan 淑春园, the Lang Runyuan 郎润园, the Ying Chunyuan 迎春园, the Zhi Deyuan 自得园, and the Le Shanyuan 乐善园.[7] The Yuan Mingyuan, extended to a much larger scale by Yong Zheng in AD 1725, was further developed by Qian Long in AD 1737.

On the west side of the Tiananmen is the Great Hall of the People. Built in 1959, it contains a banquet hall for over five thousand, a concert hall for ten thousand, the hall where Mao Zedong's body lay in state and where the National People's Congress takes place. It has ornately decorated coffered ceilings and columns.

To the east of Tiananmen Square is the Museum of National History which was constructed in 1959. The museum houses exhibits that trace the history of China. In the south part of Tiananmen Square are the Monument of the People's Heroes and the Memorial Hall of Mao Zedong. The former, dated 1958, stands on a 3,000-square-metre terrace, and symbolises the heroic struggle and triumph of the revolutionaries. It is a granite obelisk almost 38 metres in height, carved with red stars, pines and cypresses to signify that the spirit of the martyrs will live on. Around the plinth of the obelisk are eight marble slabs carved in relief to depict scenes from Chinese historical events.

The Memorial Hall is oriented to the north and it houses the embalmed body of

Mao Zedong. It is raised on a two-tiered podium which is encircled by marble balustrades. The two-tiered roof is supported by forty-eight octagonal granite columns. The roof is covered with gold glazed tiles. Contemporary sculptures of revolutionaries decorate the south gate. The Hall is surrounded by the landscaped garden which contains many species of trees and plants.

The Museum of the Chinese Revolution and the Museum of Chinese History, covering an area of 65,000 square metres, are housed in one building situated on the east of the Tiananmen. This building has many levels and contains a two-level exhibition hall with 4,000 square metres of exhibition space. The permanent exhibits reveal the historical events of the socialist revolution.

The Museum of Chinese History presents many relics and ancient documents which reveal the historical development of China. It is organised in four main sections to relate the various stages of development of Chinese society – the primitive, the slave, the feudal and the democratic revolutionary society. Some other areas exhibit Chinese antiques and instruments from the Tang dynasty right down to the present time. One section shows Chinese paintings and historical documents.

The most outstanding architectural monuments in the inner city are the former palaces of the Zi Jincheng which are now named the Gugong Powu Yuan 故宫博物院 or Palace Museum.[8] From AD 1420 to 1911 the Gugong was the administrative and political centre as well as the residential palaces of the imperial rulers. After the Nationalists had taken over the government and Pu Yi, the last emperor of the Qing dynasty, had resigned the Gugong was turned into an Exhibition Hall, but Pu Yi and his wives were allowed to stay in the inner palaces. In AD 1925 Pu Yi and his family were driven out of the palaces and the Palace Museum was set up. In AD 1949 the People's Republic of China liberated the country from the Nationalists and had the Palace Museum renovated and declared a national monument.

The outer city and suburbs of Beijing contain a few outstanding monuments such as the Tiantan 天坛 (the Temple of Heaven) in the south, the Yi Heyuan (the Summer Palace) in the northwest, the Ming tombs to the north and the Great Wall of China.[9]

The Tiantan is entered through its west gate from which the triple-tiered white marble mound, the Qi Niandian 祈年殿 and the other structures can be seen. Two prominent universities are sited at the northwestern side of the outer city. One is the Beijing University and the other, the Qinghua University.[10] There are other important buildings outside the Gugong such as the Beijing Library and the Working People's Palace of Culture.[11] The latter was in fact the imperial ancestor worship temple complex, originally named Tai Maio 太庙, built by Yong Le, the Ming emperor. It consists of three temple halls.[12] The first was formerly named Da Jimen and its elevation is designed in five bays. The imperial ancestor worship halls were turned into a museum in AD 1950.

Of the many temples in Beijing, the majority are Buddhist and a great number of these have long historical records dating back to the Jin dynasty. For example, the Guang Jisi 广济寺 was first constructed during the Jin period. It went through glorious as well as difficult times. It was burnt, destroyed and rebuilt in AD 1935. It is now the headquarters of the Buddhist Society in Beijing. Its plan is based on the courtyard concept and its construction follows that of the traditional style of Chinese architecture. The main prayer hall is named Daxiong Baodian 大雄宝殿 as it houses the main Buddhist deities such as the Buddha and the Eighteen Luohan 罗汉 (arhats).

The Fa Yuansi 法原寺 temple, which also has a rich historical background, was built in AD 645 by the Tang emperor, Tai Zong 太宗. The construction was under the supervision of the empress Wu Zetian 武则天. Its original structure was destroyed by the Liaos and its present form was built by Qing emperor, Yong Zheng.

One of Beijing's more interesting temples is the Bi Yunsi 碧云寺. Built in the Yuan dynasty, it stands on the undulating ground of the east slopes of the western hills. The entrance bridge over the valley of the stream is dramatic. From the entrance the ground level begins to rise and the highest point is terminated by the Diamond Throne Pagoda. The temple is based on the courtyard plan with a series of courtyards and halls.

Another temple sited on the western hill slopes is the Wo Fosi 卧佛寺, built during the Tang dynasty. Its name relates to a huge copper statue of Buddha housed within. Since the Tang dynasty it has been renovated several times. Older than the Wo Fosi is the Buddhist temple, Tan Tuosi 潭拓寺, situated in the hills of Men Tougou, west of Beijing. Tan Zhesi was built in the Jin dynasty. Ten kilometres away is the Jie Tasi 阶太寺 which dates back to the Tang dynasty.

Right in the city centre is a Lama temple named Yong Hegong. This temple has an interesting historical background as it was originally the residential palace of Yong He before he ascended the throne. Also in the city centre of Beijing are many churches, mosques, arts and crafts centres.

The Central Institute for Nationalities, established in AD 1949, offers training programmes and courses to students on politics, languages, literature, mathematics and sciences.

Since becoming the capital of the Yuan dynasty, Beijing has gained recognition as one of the world's largest and most important cities. It is now the capital of China and an important industrial city as well as a major centre of trade and culture. It contains countless international commercial headquarters, hundreds of new housing projects, fifty museums, eighty-three institutions of higher learning, three hundred and twenty publishing houses, five hundred scientific research establishments and numerous parks and monuments. It is also a religious centre with numerous magnificent temples, mosques and churches. Its international airport was completed in AD 1979 and since then it has become a meeting place for people from all over the world.

Notes

1 See map on p10 for the location of Beijing and on p88 for the locations of gardens in Beijing.

2 The fossil remains of a Beijing man, a primitive cave man, was found in Zhou Kuodian 周口店, at the southwest of Beijing.

3 See Kaplan, Fredric, and Keijzer, Arne, *The China Guidebook*, Eurasia Press, Inc (New York) 1982, pp192-194. See also Liu Junwen, *Beijing, China's Ancient and Modern Capital*, Foreign Languages Press (Beijing) 1982, p4.

4 The outstanding monument left by the Jin is the Lu Gouqiao 芦沟桥, the bridge that spans over the Yong Dinghe 永定河. The bridge, 266 by 9.3 metres, is magnificently detailed with two hundred and eighty balusters decorated with lion sculptures.

5 See Pan Guxi 潘谷西, *Zhong Guo Jian Zhu* 中国建筑, Zhong Guo Jian Zhu Gongye Chuban She 中国建筑工业出版社 (Beijing) 1982, p48.

6 There were many changes in Beijing from the Jin to the Qing dynasty.

7 See diagrams on p88 for the locations of gardens during the reigns of Kang Xi (coloured black) and Qian Long (dotted).

8 See section on Zi Jincheng on pp46-59.

9 See sections on the Tiantan on pp79-81 and the Summer Palace on pp93-99. The Great Wall of China was built by seven hundred thousand labourers at the order of Qinshi Huangdi 秦始皇帝 who reigned from 211-206 BC and united China. The Ming Tombs were the royal burial ground of thirteen Ming emperors. They were designed by emperor Yong Le. The approach was by spirit way and through a five-arch entrance gate. After passing a red gate, pavilion and crossing a bridge, the first tomb, of Yong Le, is reached. Each tomb is elaborately planned with an individual gate and wall enclosures. To enter the burial barrow one has to go through another gate. An elaborate altar and tall tower were built in front of the barrow.

10 The Beijing University is to the northwest of the Gugong. Founded in AD 1898 it has a rich historical background and past administrators and lecturers include well-known educationalists such as Cai Yuanpei 蔡元培 and Luxun 鲁迅. The Qinghua University is designed around the courtyard concept. Established in AD 1911 it is well known as an educational and academic centre for eminent scholars all over the world, its past educationalists include Liu Xianzhou 刘仙洲 and Liang Sicheng 梁思成.

11 The Beijing Library is China's national library containing almost ten million volumes of books. It is a classical building covered by a green glazed tile roof and enclosed by a red wall.

12 The building compound covers an area of 130,000 square metres.

The Gugong of Beijing

Situated in the heart of Beijing the Gugong 故宫 (the Palace Museum) has served twenty-four emperors since AD 1420 as their imperial palaces and administration centre. Within a walled enclosure of 1,005 metres by 758 metres surrounded by a moat, the Tong Zihe 筒子河, it was first built by the Ming ruler, emperor Yong Le 永乐 (AD 1403–424) in the seventh lunar month of AD 1406. Yong Le promoted Cheng Gui 陈桂 to be the chief construction supervisor of his imperial palaces. Cheng Gui was to be assisted by Wang Tong 王通 and Liu Sheng 柳升. Constructed like a city within a city the imperial palace complex was to be sited on an area within the Huangcheng 皇城 (royal city) covering over seven hectares of land in the capital city, Beijing. In AD 1407 Cheng Gui and his assistants gathered all the skilled craftsmen and builders who were familiar with the building techniques elaborated in the *Yingzao Fashi* 营造法式 to build the Gugong.[1] When the Gugong was completed it was named Zi Jincheng 紫禁城 (Forbidden City). *Zi* 紫 represented the ever shining constellation, Zi Huixing 紫徽星 (the North Star). The city was forbidden to the ordinary man and no one was to enter it without permission from the royal household. Site work and construction of the palaces finally started in AD 1420.

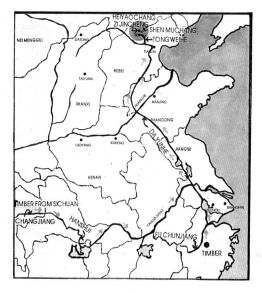

The best materials were ordered for the construction of the city and palaces. All structural materials were good-quality hardwood brought in along the rivers from Zhijiang 浙江, Hubei 河北 and Hunan 河南.[2] Over eighty million bricks of the best quality were used to build the walls within the city. The stonework, mainly marble, was obtained from the nearby quarries in Beijing 北京 and from Quyang 曲阳. Terracotta and glazed tiles were fired in kilns specially built in Beijing at that time to meet the demand of the builders of the Gugong in the Forbidden City. Over one hunded thousand builders and workers were on the site to build the imperial city which then contained over nine thousand nine hundred and ninety-nine rooms and spaces. The lack of natural water courses required bringing water from the Tai Yeci 太液池 (a lake to the northwest). The concept of planning of the city was based on 'zuo zhu you she' 左祖右社 (having the ancestor worship hall on the left and the shrine for the god of earth on the right). Thus in front of the main gate, the Wumen 午门, the Tai Miao 太庙 (temple for Ancestor Worship) and the She Jitan 社稷堂 (temple for the Worship of the God of Earth) were built.

The former imperial palace complex was designed with multiple lines of defence as it was an imperial city within the inner city of Beijing. The imperial palace complex was surrounded by a 10-metre-high wall and the city by a walled enclosure. The main gate of the city was named Qianmen 前门 or Zheng Yangmen 正阳门 and the main gate to the imperial city was the Tiananmen 天安门 beyond which is the Duanmen 端门. The main exits were the Dianmen 殿门 (for city) and the Shen Wumen 神武门 (for imperial city). At each corner of the imperial wall enclosure is an uniquely designed three-storey watch tower.[3] Beyond the wall enclosure is the Tong Zihe 筒子河, a 52-metre-wide moat. The imperial palace complex was to be entered through four main gateways. The Wumen 午门 in the south, the Shen Wumen

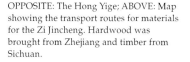

OPPOSITE: The Hong Yige; ABOVE: Map showing the transport routes for materials for the Zi Jincheng. Hardwood was brought from Zhejiang and timber from Sichuan.

The three-tier marble podium of the Tai Hedian facing Qian Qinggong displays many gargoyles of hornless dragon heads through which surface water is drained.

The Wumen is also known as Wu Fenglou, an auspicious name which means the Gateway of Five Phoenix. It has a u-shaped plan enclosing a paved courtyard. Structural elements are brilliantly painted in blue and red and the wall panels are intricate timber latticework.

The beautifully painted tiers of beams in the upper section of the Wumen, contrast vividly with the red columns. The elegant interlocking *dougong*, painted predominantly green and blue, appear decorative, but support the cantilevered eaves and verge overhangs. Nine mythical animals terminate the roof corners to repel bad fortune.

The Wai and Neijin Shuihe symbolise wealth and good *qi* being brought into the imperial household. The Neijin Shuiqiao is in front of the Tai Hemen and is crossed by the five bridges shown here.

神午门 in the north, one in the east called Dong Huamen 东华门 and one in the west named Xi Huamen 西华门. The imperial palaces were oriented south because it was considered an auspicious orientation for the emperor as he met the gaze of the heavens. The North Star behind the most important buildings had to be on the central axial line which was an extension of the Heavenly Meridian. So the planning of the Gugong is based on symmetry, walled enclosures, the courtyard concept and also on the planning concept of 'qian chao hou qin' 前朝后寝 (placing the public audience halls at the front and the private halls for resting at the rear). The public halls for administration are named the Tai Hedian 太和殿 (the Hall of Supreme Harmony), the Zhong Hedian 中和殿 (the Central Hall of Harmony) and the Bao Hedian 保和殿 (the Hall of Protection and Harmony).[4] To reach these palaces a progression through a hierarchy of spaces and through a series of important gateways and courtyards has to be made. The entrance to the former imperial palace ground is through the Tiananmen 天安门 which is reached by crossing the Waijin Shuiqiao 外金水桥 (Outer Golden Water Bridge). The Waijin Shuiqiao is made up of five bridges. The middle bridge, Yu Luqiao 御路桥, was used solely by the emperor. It is guarded by a pair of hou 猴 (believed to be the ninth son of a dragon). Tiananmen was constructed in AD 1417 during the reign of emperor Yong Le 永乐. It was first named Cheng Tianmen 承天门 but collapsed several times. It was later rebuilt by emperor Shun Zhi 顺治 in AD 1651 and it was then given its present name. It was used only by specific people and on certain occasions. For example, when the emperor chose and named his empress the announcement would be made at the Tiananmen. On the other hand when he led his army to fight a war he would go through this gateway. However, no funeral procession, not even the emperor's, was allowed through the Tiananmen.

Beyond the Tiananmen is a courtyard which is enclosed on the sides by covered walkways. The second entrance is called Duanmen 端门. Beyond it is an elongated courtyard which is flanked by covered walkways and four side entrances – She Zuomen 社左门, Miao Youmen 庙右门, Que Zuomen 阙左门 and Que Youmen 阙右门.

Entrance to the first courtyard of the Gugong Palace Museum is through the Wumen 午门 (the south gate) which was twice restored in AD 1647 and 1801 respectively. This elaborate u-shaped entrance consists of nine halls on a podium over 10 metres high. Three main and two side doors lead to the Wumen, each serving a special purpose. The main central door was used exclusively by the emperor. The empress could use it only once in her life time and that was on the day of her wedding. Those who won the top three honours of the annual imperial examinations of the Qing dynasty were also allowed to enter it only once in their lifetime when they were interviewed by the emperor. During the Qing dynasty it was customary for the emperor to distribute the lunar calendars to distinguished subjects in the tenth lunar month at the main gate of the Wumen. At the end of the lunar new year celebrations, a lantern festival would be held at the Wumen in his presence. One of the main doors on the east side was used by the emperor's ministers and top officials. The other main door on the west was used by his relatives. The side doors were used before sunrise by government officials and generals who had to attend imperial audiences.[5]

The second entrance is called the Tai Hemen 太和门. In the courtyard between the Wumen and Tai Hemen is the Jin Shuiqiao (five marble bridges) which spans over the Golden Water Stream which originates at the Jade Fountain Spring near the Summer Palace.[6] The distance between the Wumen and Tai Hemen is 160 metres.

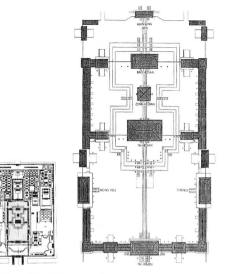

Roof plan of the Zi Jincheng showing the roof forms and layout of the central palaces

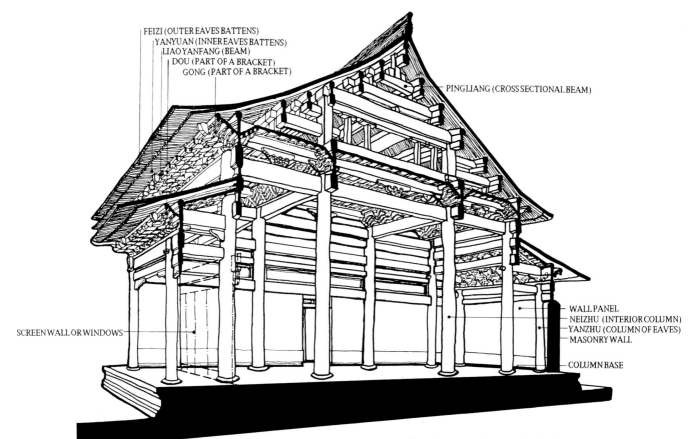

FEIZI (OUTER EAVES BATTENS)
YANYUAN (INNER EAVES BATTENS)
LIAO YANFANG (BEAM)
DOU (PART OF A BRACKET)
GONG (PART OF A BRACKET)

PINGLIANG (CROSS SECTIONAL BEAM)

SCREEN WALL OR WINDOWS

WALL PANEL
NEIZHU (INTERIOR COLUMN)
YANZHU (COLUMN OF EAVES)
MASONRY WALL

COLUMN BASE

Three-dimensional section showing the
structural elements of the Tai Hedian

The throne of Tai Hedian is in the main hall
where majestic columns 12 metres high, six of
which are gilded with dynamic dragon images,
support ceilings of elaborate green and gold
caissons painted with dancing dragons. In a
domed recess in the central bay, sits a superb
golden dragon sculpture complete with a
pendant of celestial pearls. The throne of
the former ruler, the seat, table, screen and
ornaments, built of *nanmu*, are most
elaborately carved and exquisitely designed.

Based on the theme of 'qian zhao hou chen' the most important hall is the Tai Hedian which presides over the vast courtyard where thousands used to kneel whenever the Qing emperor held audiences with his ministers, his warriors and other subjects. It was used mainly for important events such as coronations of emperors, royal marriage ceremonies and celebrations of the emperors' birthday. The entry to Tai Hedian is through the Tai Hemen 太和门 (the Door of Supreme Harmony) which has nine colonnades standing on a stone podium and is guarded by a pair of bronze lions.[7] As mentioned earlier, beyond this gateway is a large 30,000-square-metre courtyard which could house about ninety thousand people during important public functions.

Beyond the courtyard is the Tai Hedian 太和殿. Built in AD 1421, it was subjected to two fires and renovated in AD 1669 and 1765.[8] The most impressive building in the Gugong, it measures over 63 metres in length, 37 metres in width and almost 30 metres in height, and it stands on a 7-metre-high podium.[9] It is covered by a two-tiered hipped roof with substantial eaves and verge overhangs supported by intricate dougong (brackets).[10] Its magnificent roofs are covered with yellow glazed tiles and its roof ridge is terminated with dragon heads. Internally it is finished with various coffered and intricately ornamental ceilings with yin (green pearls) and yang (golden dragons) colours and symbols. Each coffered ceiling is framed by beams skilfully painted in green and gold of various shades. Its eleven-bay facade and walls are mainly red in colour and its doors and windows elaborately carved. The central columns (14.4 metres high and 1 metre in diameter) are gilded with entwined dragons. The side columns are bright red contrasting vividly with the beams and coffered panels of the ceiling which have patterns of gilded dancing dragons on a green background.

The interior of the hall is filled with bronze incense burners, intricately carved wooden screens, gilded copper cauldrons and many other treasures. The throne is placed on the central axial line on a raised dais or platform which is 2 metres high. The gilded baozuo 宝座 (imperial seat) is exquisitely designed and is flanked by precious jadeware on tripods. In front of the imperial seat is a gilded table intricately carved with dragons flanking the celestial pearl. Behind the baozuo is a seven-panelled pingfeng 屏风 (screen) which is most ornamental with dragons carved in dynamic poses. Ornamental and precious objects such as the bronze cranes (representing longevity), the elephant-shaped incense burner (symbolising wisdom) and the tripods shaped like mythical animals (representing power) are placed around the throne.

The second hall is the Zhong Hedian which was built in AD 1420 and, like the Tai Hedian, suffered two fires.[11] Restored in AD 1627 and 1765, it was used by the former emperor as a temporary place of rest and relaxation between periods of holding audience with his subjects. In this hall the Qing dynasty emperor used to examine rice grains, fruit seeds and other natural produce. He also received members of the cabinet and officials of the ministry in this palace. The hall is square in shape and its roof is covered with a magnificent pyramidal roof which tilts gently upwards. The roof ridge corners carry seven mythical animal symbols.[12] It houses a throne and precious objects such as incense burners and tripods.

The third hall is the Bao Hedian which was used by the emperor to prepare himself before holding an audience with his subjects.[13] The Bao Hedian was also used by the emperor for interviewing the scholars who had passed the annual imperial examinations. It was then customary for the emperor to pass the final judgement on the winning scholars before the top three honours were awarded. It was also where the emperor received tribute-bearing envoys from vassal territories. This imperial

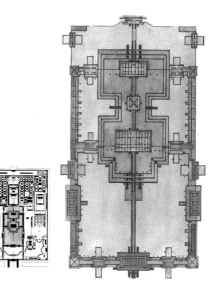

Plan of the three main palaces of the Zi Jincheng

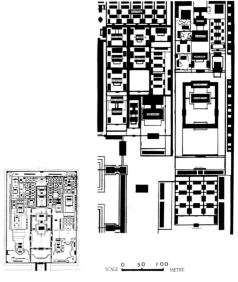

SCALE 0   50   100   METRE

Block layout of the eastern palaces

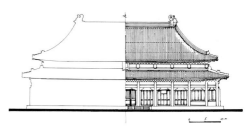

Part elevation of the Tai Hedian, the Hall of Supreme Harmony, which was the most important building in the Forbidden City during the Qing dynasty. The eleven corner rib ornaments and the yellow tiles of its two-tiered hipped roof reflect the supreme power of the emperor. Powerful motifs were engraved and carved on the spirit ways and marble balustrades as well as painted on the coffered ceilings.

The Tai Hemen, oriented south, is flanked by walls and side entrances covered by half-hipped/half-gabled roofs. In front of the Tai Hemen are the marble balustrades of the Neijin Shuiqiao.

The approach to the magnificent Tai Hedian, is a grand flight of stairs divided by the imperial path, over which the Qing emperor was carried in a sedan chair whenever he entered or left the hall.

Within a simple interior, the imperial throne of Zhong Hedian is on a raised platform covered with a green carpet and sits behind a golden coloured screen. Delicate latticework screens the windows.

The Bao Hedian, seen behind the Zhong Hedian, was the main banqueting hall of the emperor. It is 29 metres high and has an area of 1,240 square metres.

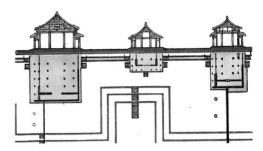

palace suffered the same fate as the other palaces, the Tai Hedian and the Zhong Hedian, as it was destroyed by fire and had to be rebuilt.

A magnificent building standing on a podium, the Bao Hedian is covered by a two-tiered half-hipped/half-gabled roof of yellow glazed tiles. Its yellow roof ridge is beautifully terminated by *wenshou* 吻兽 that resemble fish-dragon heads. The upper roof sails above the jade-green clerestory. The nine-bay elevation is made more three-dimensional by the set-back of the wall and door panels which are in green and red. The doors are intricately detailed and built. The free-standing bright red columns with green brackets support jade-green longitudinal beams that are beautifully patterned with auspicious symbols.

The interior of the Bao Hedian contains a throne raised six steps above the internal floor level. The *baozuo* is golden in colour depicting the power of the imperial ruler. Ornaments and artefacts are decorated with gilded carving and dragon motifs. The structural columns are red in colour. Its coffered ceiling panels are red, gold and green and patterned with auspicious symbols such as dragons and pearls. A three-tier staircase flanking a central imperial ramp leads from the Bao Hedian to the internal courtyard below. The ramp, used when the emperor was carried in his sedan chair, is a 16-metre monolithic white marble slab carved with dragons and clouds to signify the supreme power of the emperor. The weight of the marble is over two hundred tons.

Part plan and section of the Tai Hedian, the Zhong Hedian and the Bao Hedian.

Constructed of jade-like marble slabs laid out as the Chinese character *gong*, the marble podium of the Tai Hedian has intricate white marble balustrades with baluster heads of dragons and phoenix which are water spouts.

As stated earlier, during the Qing dynasty, the Zi Jincheng contained the *waichao* 外朝 and the *neichao* 内朝. At one time there were nine thousand nine hundred and ninety-nine-and-a-half enclosed spaces in the Zi Jincheng![14] The *waichao* was for public administration while the *neichao* for residence and private use. The main portion of the *neichao* is the area where the emperor used to reside and prepare himself before a public audience. It can be roughly divided into three main areas: three main palaces in the centre, six to the east and six to the west. These are named '*sangong liuyuan*' 三宫六苑 (three palace complexes and six courtyards). Entrance to the central group of residential palaces is through the Qian Qingmen 乾清门 which is guarded by two gilded bronze lions.[15] This group of buildings consists of the Qian Qinggong 乾清宫, the Kun Ninggong 坤宁宫, the Jiao Taidian 交泰殿, the Zhao Rendian 昭仁殿, the Hong Dedian 宏德殿, the Qin Andian 钦安殿 and some other minor halls. The Qian Qinggong 乾清宫, Jiao Taidian 交泰殿 and the Kun Ninggong 坤宁宫 were built for the residence of the royal family and so were placed along the central axial line of the city. The Qian Qinggong was originally built as the residential palace for the emperor and the empress in AD 1420. After emperor Shun Zhi's 顺治 body was placed in repose waiting for an auspicious date for his burial it was never used as a residence.[16] The facade of this two-storey building is divided into nine bays to signify *yang* power. Before Shun Zhi's death he used it as his bedroom. Three beds were placed in each bedroom so that there were twenty-seven beds in nine bedrooms. The emperor was supposed to change his bed every night so that would-be assassins did not know where he was sleeping on a particular night.

There is a huge signboard with the words '*Zheng Da Guang Ming*' 正大光明 hanging in the palace hall. Since the era of emperor Qian Long, the appointment of the crown prince was kept secret, only revealed on reading the emperor's will. This was kept in a small safe on top of the signboard. Upon the death of the emperor the will would be taken down and read by the chief minister. The surrounding terraces of the Qian Qinggong are decorated with gilded incense burners, miniature temple models, bronze tortoises and other precious objects such as the sundial and grain-measuring equipment.

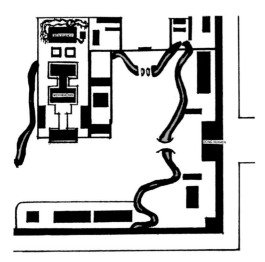

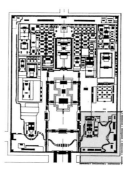

SCALE 0 50 100 METRE

Block layout of the southeastern palaces

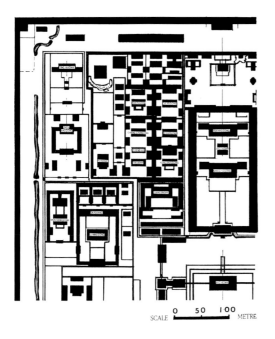

SCALE 0 50 100 METRE

Block layout of the western palaces

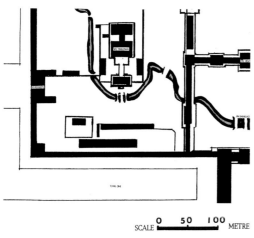

SCALE 0 50 100 METRE

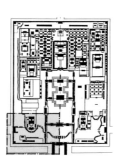

Block layout of the southwestern palaces

The Jiao Taidian was built for the Qing empress to hold audiences with her royal family members and it was also used by the emperor on his birthday to receive his royal guests. The imperial seals were once kept here.

The Kun Ninggong was built in AD 1440 for the Qing royal family to meet with the former Qing empress. During the Qing dynasty this palace was used by the emperor and the empress for their wedding. It burnt down in AD 1514 and was rebuilt in 1519.

Some of the residential and private halls for the Qing emperor and his family are situated at the east and west sides of the complex. The eastern palaces are: the Zhaigong 斋宫, the Cheng Xiaodian 诚肃殿, the Jing Rengong 景仁宫, Cheng Qiangong 承乾宫, the Zhong Cuigong 钟粹宫, the Yong Hegong 永和宫, the Jing Yanggong 景阳宫 and some other minor palaces. To the further east part of the complex are: the Huang Jidian 皇极殿, the Ning Shougong 宁寿宫, the Yang Xindian 养心殿, the Le Shoutang 乐寿堂, the Yi Hexuan 颐和轩, the Jing Qige 景棋阁, the Jing Fugong 景福宫 and other minor halls such as the Fan Hualou 梵华楼.

The Zhaigong was used by the emperor to rest, fast and meditate before the offering of prayers for the new year. The Cheng Xiaodian was linked to the Zhaigong. The Zhong Cuigong was built for the crown prince of emperor Kang Xi, the Chen Qiangong, the Jing Rengong and the Yong Hegong to store priceless treasures while the Yang Xindian was used by the supreme ruler, the emperor, as his residence.

The Jing Yanggong was for the storage of fine art, literature and other treasures of the powerful royal household. The Huang Jidian was connected to the Ning Shougong which was used for the practice of rituals and when Qian Long retired he spent the rest of his life there. The Yu Jinggong was the residence of the crown prince.

South of the eastern palaces are the Nan Sansuo 南山所 which consisted of the imperial kitchen, the hall for the imperial doctors, the dispensary and the store for tea leaves. The Nan Sansuo was renovated in AD 1766. There are two unusual walls at the north and south of this group of buildings. One is called the *qiu longpi* 九龙壁 and the other the *yingpi* 影壁.

East of the Tai Hemen is a group of palaces which includes the Wen Huadian 文华殿 and the Wen Yuange 文渊阁. The Wen Huadian was the palace of the prince of the Ming dynasty while the Wen Yuange was the largest imperial library. It is covered with a half-hipped/half-gabled purplish-black glazed tile roof because it was believed that black, being a Water Element was able to control the outbreak of fire (Fire Element). This two-storey library housed the *siku quanshu* 四库全书 (the complete collection of the Four Treasures of Knowledge).[17] The collection consisted of almost eighty thousand volumes. Besides these there were three thousand four hundred books in the library.

The major western palaces are: the Yang Xindian 养心殿, the Yong Shougong 永寿宫, the Tai Jidian 太极殿, the Chang Chungong 长春宫, the Yi Kungong 翊坤宫, the Tai Hedian 体和殿, the Chu Xiugong 储秀宫, the Tong Daotang 同道堂, the Yu Huage 雨花阁, the Ying Huadian 英华殿, the Shou Angong 寿安宫, the Ci Ninggong 慈宁宫, the Da Fotang 大佛堂 and other minor halls.

The Yang Xindian, the Yong Shougong and many of the palaces were for residential use. The former was used by several emperors as their residence. The Yu Huage and the Da Fotang were temples for prayers. The Chu Xiugong, the Yong Shougong and the Yi Kungong were residential palaces for the emperor's concubines. The Chang Chungong was the residential palace for Cixi when she was the concubine of emperor Xian Feng 咸丰 (AD 1851–1862). The Yin Huadian was once a Lamaist temple.

South of the western palaces the Wu Yingdian 武英殿, and some other halls were built. Wu Yingdian was a hall where the emperor would receive military personalities.

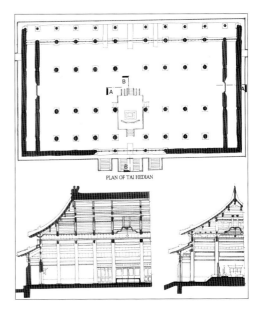

Plan and part sections of the Tai Hedian

Built during the Ming dynasty as a place of rest for the Qing emperor, Yong Zheng, the front of the Yang Xindian was used for administration while the rear was his residence. The ornately finished interior has caisson panels around a domed gilded ceiling.

Two of the most ornately built pavilions in the imperial garden, the Qian Qiuting, shown here, and the Ling Xiangting, have extremely elaborate roofs.

In the Gugong a total of eight thousand seven hundred enclosed spaces are still in existence. All the buildings are grouped in the *si heyuan* 四合院 style (courtyard concept). The roof forms are basically hipped, gabled, half-hipped/half-gabled and pyramidal. The most important building has the highest number of tiers on its hipped roof and is placed on the central axial line of the Gugong.

The Zi Jincheng is enclosed with a high wall and at each corner of the enclosure is an imposing tower pavilion. This pavilion is covered with an interesting multi-level, multi-directional glazed tile roof. Beyond the enclosing walls is the Tong Zihe 筒子河 which was built as a means of security.

All the palaces were built with the finest building materials. Three types of bricks were employed: *chengzhuan* 城砖 for building podiums; *cheng jiangzhuan* 澄浆砖 being of fine texture, as finish paving; *fangzhuan* 方砖 for interior floors and covered corridors. Three types of glazed tiles were used for the roofs. For the imperial halls yellow glazed tiles of the finest quality were used.

Details of roof eaves of Qian Qiuting showing the cantilevered eaves and roof edge tiles

Beyond the minor palaces are Qing imperial gardens which are landscaped with hundreds of fine trees and species of plants. At the north of the Forbidden City is the most significant imperial garden, the Yu Huayuan 御花园, built by Qian Long. The main gateway of the entrance to this garden named Tian Yimen 天一门 is built of grey bricks on a marble podium. It is covered with a yellow glazed tile roof and is guarded by a pair of gilded unicorns. The east and west entrances are the Yan Hemen 延和门 and Jifume 集福门 respectively. The main building in the garden, the Qin Andian 钦安殿, is placed on the central axial line. This building is a Taoist temple with a gilded magic vase at the centre of the ridge and it divides the garden into east and west. To the east are several pavilions namely the Ning Xiangting 凝香亭, the Chi Zaotang 澡堂, the Yu Jingting 御景亭, the Jing Biting 净碧亭, the Wan Chunting 万春亭, the Jiang Xuexuan 绛雪轩 and the Jingting 井亭. The most interesting structure is the Jiang Xuexuan whose plan is cross-shaped and roof is covered with yellow glazed tiles. Its round lantern uses yellow glazed tiles at the upper level and is terminated with an umbrella-like ornament. Ancient trees, trees with roots inter-twined and pavements of pebbles in endlessly varied patterns all add to the courtyards' charm.[18] At the north of the Ning Xiangting is the Yu Jingting 御景亭 which is raised high on a huge sculptured rockery. Built during the Ming dynasty the terrace of this pavilion is bounded by marble balustrades. Its beams are ornately detailed and its roof is a square pyramid covered with yellow glazed tiles.

On the west are the Yang Huige 延晖阁, the Yu Cuiting 玉春亭, the Cheng Ruiting 澄瑞亭, the Qian Qiuting 千秋亭, the Si Shenci 四神祠, the Yang Xingzhai 养性斋 and the Luyou 鹿囿. The Yang Xinzai was used by emperor Guang Xu 光绪 as a study and it was beautifully landscaped. The Qian Qiuting is similar to the Jiang Xuexuan in terms of planning and construction.

Opposite the exit gateway of the Forbidden City is the Jingshan 景山 or Coal Hill.[19] Situated north of the imperial palaces it affords an excellent panoramic view. The 46-metre high hill is crowned with five peaks and on each peak stands a pavilion. The central pavilion, Wan Chunting 万春亭, is covered with a three-tiered roof. Due west of the Coal Hill is the Beihai Park which dates back to AD 300. In the park are three man-made lakes – the Beihai 北海, the Zhonghai 中海 and the Nanhai 南海. The Beihai was deepened during the Jin dynasty (twelfth century AD). At the early part of the eleventh century the emperor had his residential quarters there. Zhi Chunqiao 知春桥 (bridge of perfect wisdom) was built to link an island on the Beihai to the southeast side. It affords distant views of the north shore and the Wu Longting 五龙亭 or Five Dragon Pavilion. The Wu Longting are built over the Beihai lake from where the white Dagoba can be seen. The Baita or Dagoba 白塔 was built on the island to commemorate a Lama monk.

The planning and architecture of Gugong can be summed up as follows:

• The Gugong, a significant example of symmetrical planning of balance and harmony, was built to demonstrate imperial power in physical form.

• The palace complex, based on the concept of *si heyuan* reflects the Chinese concepts of *yin* and *yang* and feudalistic system.

• The expression of the roof forms of the palaces spells the Chinese system of hierarchy of power and importance in the following sequence: two-tier hipped roof, two-tier half-hipped/half-gabled roof, two-tier pyramidal roof, hipped roof, half-hipped/half-gabled roof, pyramidal roof, and gabled roof.

• The importance of a building is also indicated by the colour scheme of the walls and roofs in the following sequence: yellow, red, green, blue, black and grey. The roofs of the imperial palaces are yellow while roofs of less distinguished buildings are green.

Indeed, the buildings in the Gugong were meant to be structures used by rulers with supreme power. They were designed with reference to physical and metaphysical forces so that they were auspicious and that those who used them would also enjoy the best of luck and health.

Notes

1 The chief stone mason was Lu Xiang 陆祥 who was the expert in stone masonry at that time. The chief roof and tile maker was Yang Chun 杨春 and the chief craftsman and timber construction expert was Kuai Xiang 蒯祥. Reference books included the *Liji* 礼记 and *Kao Gongji* 考工记.

2 The best hard wood, *nanmu* 楠木, was used for the construction of buildings. The best timber from Zhijiang was transported down the Fu Chunjiang 富春江, the Da Yunhe 大运河 through Tianjin 天津, then the Bei Yunhe 北运河 and the Wei He 惠河, and finally to Beijing.

3 All building elements were placed in accordance with traditional practices mentioned in the ancient texts.

4 The Tai Hedian, the Zhong Hedian and the Bao Hedian were constructed in AD 1421. These palaces were subjected to fire hazards in the years AD 1597, and 1758. They were rebuilt in AD 1655 and 1765 respectively. See Yu Zhuo Yun 于倬云, *Zi Jincheng Gongdian* 紫禁城宫殿, Shangwu Yingshu Guan 商务印书馆 (Hong Kong) 1982, p325.

5 See Ren Jiyu 任继愈, *Zhongguo de Mingsheng Guji* 中国的名胜古迹, Zhongguo Wenfa Shizhi Congshu 中国文法知识丛书 (Beijing) 1991, p90. It was traditional practice to have five entrances to a palace.

6 The five-arched bridge symbolises the five virtues of man namely *zhi* (intelligent), *xin* 信 (trust), *ren* 人 (benevolence), *yong* 勇 (bravery) and *yan* 严 (principle).

7 The lions were used as guardians as early as the Han dynasty when the Han emperor was presented with a pair of lions by the African chief. They were regarded as powerful animals and were symbolic of great strength. They were also presented as a pair, the male on the left holding a ball while the female sits on the right holding a cub.

8 When the Tai Hedian was completed it was named Feng Tiandian 奉天殿. Its present name was given by emperor Shun Zhi in AD 1645.

9 During the Ming and Qing eras the Tai Hedian was the tallest building in Beijing.

10 The two-tier hipped roof is for the most important building in a complex. Other two-tier roof forms in order of importance are: two-tier half-hipped/half-gabled roof and two tier pyramidal roof.

11 The Zhong Hedian was named Hua Gai 华盖 by emperor Yong Le in AD 1421. Its name changed to Zhong Jidian 中极殿 in AD 1562 and it was renamed by emperor Shun Zhi in AD 1645 as Zhong Hedian.

12 The Zhong Hedian was not as important as the Tai Hedian or the Bao Hedian because each of the latter's roof ridge corners have as many as nine mythical animal symbols. The more animal symbols the roof corners carry, the more important the building. However, the number of symbols must be an odd number (*yang*).

13 The Bao Hedian was named by emperor Yong Le as Jinshen 谨身 after it was completed in AD 1421. In AD 1562 emperor Jia Jing 嘉靖 renamed it as Jian Jidian 建极殿. It was given its present name by emperor Shun Zhi in AD 1645.

14 It was believed that there were only ten thousand palaces in the heavens and that the earthly emperor should not have as many rooms as the Emperor Above. Indeed, the lower floor of the Wen Yuange was so small in area that it only contained a staircase. In AD 1955 when the enclosed spaces in the Gugong were counted it was found that there were only eight thousand six hundred and sixty-two, as some buildings had been destroyed.

15 This entrance palace hall was where the emperor heard reports from his high officials.

16 It was believed that an auspicious place had to be chosen for the burial of the dead to ensure the well-being of his descendants. Similarly, a body was placed in repose until the most auspicious date and time for the burial (according to *feng shui* principles) was chosen.

17 See *The Forbidden City*, People's Fine Arts Publishing House (Beijing) nd, p19.

18 The pebble pavement patterns vary from floral, animal to legendary figures. One of the most interesting reveals the battle scene taken from the Battle of Changsha during the Three Kingdom era.

19 In AD 1644 rebel leader, Li Zicheng 李自成 marched into Beijing and took control. In despair the Ming emperor, Chong Zhen 崇桢 (AD 1611–1644) hanged himself in the palace garden on Coal Hill.

The Kanyu of the Gugong

Before the *kanyu* 堪輿 of the Gugong is discussed the term *kanyu* must be explained. *Kanyu* is an abstract term to represent the pseudo-physical science of climatology and geophysics. It is the art of placing, siting and orienting a building so that the building is in harmony with everything that surrounds it, and the art of finding balance in nature and harmony in the home and working environment. It addresses cultural and social issues of a particular society and makes reference to the natural, metaphysical and cosmological influences.

Scholars have long searched for the meaning and definition of *kanyu* or *feng shui*. Joseph Needham, the well-known scholar and author of *Science and Civilisation in China*, has suggested that *feng shui* is the result of the moulding influences of winds and waters. E J Eitel states that it is the rudiments of Chinese natural science. Some have defined it as the art of divination of good and bad habitats. I have explained the meaning of *kanyu* in previous works as the natural forces (wind and water) that exert influence on the physical environment of the living and working areas,[1] and have defined *kanyu* as the understanding of how the geographical features of a site and its topography affect buildings internally and externally.[2] As the old saying states: *feng shui* is the combination of '*tian ling di li ren he*' 天灵地利人和 (if the heavenly influences are auspicious, the geographical features are beneficial, and the actions of man are in harmony with the social, cultural and political situations, then the *feng shui* is auspicious).[3] This phrase consists of only six words and yet its implications are complex and significant. To enjoy '*tian ling*' requires: the understanding of the influences of cosmology on the earth; a knowledge of the way in which astronomy and astrology influence the orientation of man's dwelling; the disposition of the stars and the cycle of changes (*shang, zhong* and *xia yuan* 上中下元, each consisting of a period of 20 years);[4] the understanding of the Confucian classics, the *Yijing* or Book of Changes; the awareness of the weathering processes and the forces of nature (the wind, rain, snow, sun and tides, etc) upon buildings and their surrounding environment.[5] '*Di li*' refers to: the knowledge of magnetic fields and their effects on man; the appropriate siting of buildings to tap the *qi* or energy of the earth; and the understanding of the characteristics of various topographical and geographical features of land forms (hills, valleys, flat land and undulating land); the influences of the physical environmental factors on buildings both internally and externally; the orientation of buildings for maximum comfort and conducive physical environment. '*Ren he*' refers to man's relationship with others and to his surrounding environment and so it is affected by social, cultural and political influences.[6] The above confirms a statement I have made in my earlier publications that man's fate is governed by: *ming* 命 (fate), *yun* 运 (lucky and unlucky spells), *feng shui* 风水 (geomancy), *daode* 道德 (virtue) and *dushu* 读书 (education, experience, exposure, upbringing, cultural and social contacts, actions).

The practice of *kanyu* started in the West Han dynasty (third century BC). It was believed that the earth, being a living thing, had *qi* 气 (energy or life). How much *qi*

Chart showing the relationship between the Elements and Colours

Elements	Colours	Directions
Gold	White	West
Wood	Green	East
Water	Black	North
Fire	Red	South
Earth	Yellow	Central

The lowest part of the two-tiered hipped roof of the Tai Hedian displays nine mythical animals, a sign of its supreme importance and power.

a site has depended on its topography and its surrounding physical conditions. An undulating site with revitalising *qi* or *shengqi* 生气 is good for those who dwell on it. On the other hand a site with little *shengqi* or with *siqi* 死气 (harmful energy) would effect an undesirable influence on the dwellers.[7]

A good building site in north China is one facing south with hills behind and a lake in front, because the north winds are cold and dusty and the hills give at least some protection to the building during winter. By facing south the front gets the warmth of the sun and the view of the lake; therefore this is considered desirable. The surrounding physical features exert favourable or unfavourable effects on buildings directly or indirectly.[8] They either enhance or reduce the powerful quality of a site.

Since the Chinese believe in expressing their aspirations, beliefs, values and even status in society it is not surprising that they ensure the *kanyu* of their buildings are in order and in harmony with nature. Their traditional public, private and religious buildings conform to traditions and culture. Numerous ancient writings such as the *Lushi Chunqiu* 吕氏春秋 written in the Qin dynasty, the *Huainanzi* 淮南子 written in the West Han dynasty and the *Guanzi* 管子 record the need to make reference to the correct timing for the right action which is part of *kanyu* practice.[9]

Kanyu was first practised in China a few thousand years ago. Since then it has been incorporated into traditional Chinese architecture and into the buildings of homes and work places of both dignitaries and common folk. It was such an integral part of Chinese architecture that the principles and rudiments of building were based on its concepts of symmetry, balance, hierarchy of height, walled enclosures and auspicious orientation.[10]

The art of *kanyu* is deeply rooted in Chinese culture.[11] It involves the understanding of the Confucian classics such as the *Yijing* (the Book of Changes) and the meaning of *yin* and *yang* (the theory of negative and positive forces); the application of Chinese symbolism on buildings, the knowledge of the theory of magnetism and the understanding of the working of ecology; the grasp of the art of landscaping and garden design as well as the understanding of the technical skill in treating the interior and exterior of a building.

The Qi, Numerology and the Yin and Yang of Kanyu

The *qi* or *liqi* 理气 (the energy according to the geography of the land) of a site is assessed through the examination of the physical form of the land and the orientation of the building.[12] Using the various methods of assessment and applying the theory of *kanyu* based on the numerology of the *Yijing*, the workings of the Five Elements, the theory of *yin* and *yang* and the cosmology of the stars the *liqi* can be determined.[13] When the site is flat the assessment of *kanyu* is done by the *rifa* 日法 method which requires an assessment of the compatibility of the birthdate of the user of the building with the orientation of the site.[14]

China's ancient philosophical approach to numerology is found in the *Yijing*. The word *yi* 易 represents the changeability of the state of all things and the interaction and relation of the negative and positive qualities of things in nature. Confucius used the ancient numerals (Eight Trigrams) of negative (*yin* 阴) and positive (*yang* 阳) signs to form the sixty-four hexagrams for making reference to the Chinese system of cosmology. These numerals of the Eight Trigrams were attributed to emperor Fuxi (2852 BC).[15]

The ancient numerical symbols first discovered by Fuxi on the back of a mythical dragon-horse which came out of the Yellow River consisted of fifty-five dots which were later used to form the Eight Trigrams.[16] By multiplying the number 8, eight times the Sixty-Four Hexagrams were formed.[17] The number with one dot was considered an odd and *yang* number and the number with two dots an even and *yin* number. Thus, 1, 3, 5, 7, and 9 are *yang* and 2, 4, 6, and 8 are *yin* numbers. The number 9 is the supreme *yang* and so it is associated with the supreme ruler, the emperor. This number was applied on all buildings in the Gugong and the Tiantan as described earlier in this book.

Since ancient times the Chinese have associated the symbols of the Trigrams with Chinese numerology and astrological concepts. The Warring States of the Zhou dynasty (fifth to third century BC) developed the ancient philosophy into the more sophisticated theory of the *Yin* and *Yang* School which taught that everything in the world was interrelated and interdependent. It was believed that when *yin* combined harmoniously with *yang* there would be balance which would give rise to positive productivity and success.[18]

In the interpretation of traditional classical architecture, this concept of *yin* and *yang* is expressed in dualism in architecture. Masculine qualities are *yang* and feminine qualities are *yin*. Thus, built-up areas, sun-lit roofs, protruding structures and front elevations are *yang*, and void areas, shadowed eaves, set-back structures and rear elevations are *yin*. But when there is too much of *yang* in anything it will turn into *yin* and vice versa. For example, when a built-up area is too large it will be *yin* and when a roof eave tilts up too high it will become *yang*.[19] Anything that is too *yin* or too *yang* is imbalanced and, therefore, is undesirable.

When there is balance in an environment there is *qi* or rejuvenating energy. Thus, it is of vital importance that buildings should be correctly sited, appropriately related to surrounding buildings and balanced in construction materials and design elements. Perhaps this is the reason for the symmetrical layout of buildings in classical architecture.

The Five Elements and the Built Forms of Kanyu

Everything under the sky can be classified by its nature or element. There are five elements and they are called *Wuxing* 五行 (Five Elements, namely Gold, Wood, Water, Fire and Earth). Colours, seasons, senses, orientations and tastes are classified under the Elements. Gold is represented by West, Wood East, Water North, Fire South and Earth Central. It is important to note that the relationship of elements, orientations and numbers is not to be taken literally but rather as hidden meanings and unseen cosmological influences. It must also be stressed that the theory and balance of *yin*, *yang* and the Five Elements is central to Chinese thinking.

The Chinese equate the Five Planets with the Five Elements, so Mercury is Water, Venus Gold, Mars Fire, Jupiter Wood and Saturn Earth. The Five Planets are metaphorically correlated to the shape of the landforms which can be represented by the Five Elements. The Gold Element is round, the Wood long and string-like, the Water curved and fluid, the Fire pointed and star-like and the Earth rectangular.[20]

The theory of the Five Elements is applied to the analysis of the surrounding landforms and the building shapes with reference to the productive and counter-productive relationship of the Elements as shown overleaf.[21] The diagrams clearly show the desirable combination of various shapes and forms of building and landforms to the theory of mutual production and counter-production of the Five Elements. For example, a round building (Gold Element) can combine with a non-geometric building form (Water Element). Similarly, a rectangular block (Earth Element) is compatible with a round building (Gold Element).

Since Water is related to the north direction its source should be from the north.

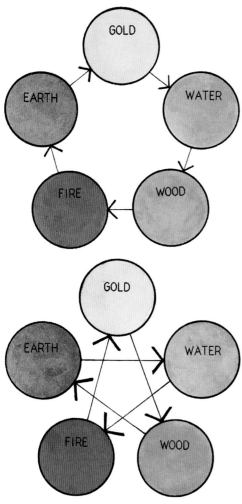

Diagrams showing the productive and destructive relationship of the Five Elements

The productive combinations are:

    Water with Wood

    Wood with Fire

    Fire with Earth

    Earth with Gold

    Gold with Water

The counter-productive combinations are:

    Earth with Water

    Water with Fire

    Fire with Gold

    Gold with Wood

    Wood with Earth

Thus, the water in the Beihai comes from the north and it is north of the Gugong. Hills in the north should also be shaped like the Water Element.

The mutual interaction of the surrounding buildings and elements affects the site favourably or unfavourably. For example, if a hill in the west has the characteristics of the Wood Element then the site is imperfect, whereas if the hill has the characteristics of the Water Element and all other features are in harmony then the site is auspicious.[22]

The Timing in Kanyu

Time is marked with sixty sexagenary cycles called *jiazi nian* 甲子年.[23] Each name of the *nian* 年 (year) consists of two Chinese characters, one from the Ten Heavenly Stems and the other from the Twelve Earthly Branches.[24] As early as the Warring States era the *yueling* 月令 diagram was created. The marking of time was based on the concept of the chronological cycle of seasons,[25] and the selection of the appropriate time for certain actions was of utter importance. For example, the commencement of construction of building works, the selecting of a time for the installation of the main ridge of a building and the selecting of a time for moving into a new building are considered very important.[26]

The most important knowledge with regards to timing is found in the Luoshu 洛书 grid. This is due to the *qi* locations changing every twenty years owing to the changes in the position of stars in the planetary system. This knowledge is incorporated in the various branches of study in *feng shui* known as Sanyuan 三元, Sanhe 三和 or Jiuxing 九星. To assess the *feng shui* of a site a *luopan* or geomancer's compass is used. Based on the Sanyuan system a *sanyuan* compass is used. This compass provides basic information and orientations related to the *Yijing*. Based on the Sanhe system a *sanhe* compass is used. This compass has three plates – the heaven, the man and the earth plates. The heaven plate divines the good and ill fortunes of man with reference to the tides. The man plate reveals the auspicious and inauspicious forces around the building and the dwelling of man. The earth plate assesses the *yin* and *yang* forces that influence the structure and dwelling. The Jiuxing method of geomancy is based on the theory that nine particular stars in the universe exert influences upon the earth. Each star has a definite route yet each is positioned at the centre of the universe at one particular time. The particular star exerts influence on man either favourably or unfavourably.

This method of divining can be worked out diagrammatically in the form of magic squares. There are nine periods or cycles of timing; each period is named a *yuan* and covers a time span of twenty years. For example, from 1864 to 1883 is the first period or cycle, 1984 to 2003 is the seventh cycle, 2004 to 2023 is in the eighth cycle and 2024 to 2043 is the ninth cycle. The first cycle starts again in 2044 and lasts until 2063. The first sixty-year period (consisting of three cyclical twenty-year-periods) is named *shangyuan* 上元 (from 1864–1923), the second sixty-year period (from 1924–1983) is called *zhongyuan* 中元 and the third *xiayuan* 下元 (from 1984–2043). Three periods of *yuan* make up the Sanyuan 三元 which lasts a total of one hundred and eighty years. Each twenty-year period is associated with a magic number of *yun*. For example, the present era, as mentioned before, has the magic number 7, *qiyun* 七云, attached to it and the assessment of the orientation of buildings may be made by the application of the magic square of 7. (Refer to the magic squares of the various eras on p68.)

When the Jiuxing method is applied to the art of placement it is important to note the date of completion of the building and Elements of the Essences of the Stars.[27] The influence of the stars on the well-being of man and the assessment of the orientation is to be read with the magic diagram of the building complete with all relevant information such as the compatibility of the Elements of the Essence of the Stars (refer to the diagrams and examples given on p68).

Chart Showing the Essence of the Stars and their Elements

Essence of Stars		Element		Period	Magic Number of Yun
1 yibai	一白	Water		1864–1883	1
2 erhei	二黑	Earth		1884–1903	2
3 sanbi	三碧	Wood		1904–1923	3
4 silu	四绿	Wood		1924–1943	4
5 wuwang	五黄	Earth		1944–1963	5
6 liubai	六白	Gold		1964–1983	6
7 qichi	七赤	Gold		1984–2003	7
8 babai	八白	Earth		2004–2023	8
9 jiuzi	九紫	Fire		2024–2043	9

It is equally important to note the numbers of the Essence of the Stars because if the yun or cycle is one (for example in the year 1684) the numbers of the Essence of the Stars are auspicious when they are 1 (meaning the expected fortune is realised within a short time) and 3 (Water and Wood are compatible Elements). The numbers of the Essence of the Stars would be inauspicious if they were 4 and 5 because the fourth cycle is quite distant from 1 and their Elements are incompatible.

The magic diagrams on pages 68 and 70 show some examples of seventh yun buildings oriented with reference to the stars. From the analysis it can be concluded that Building A is inauspicious while building B is auspicious. Unit A is oriented to face northwest and its main entrance has the star Essence of 2 and 3. The Elements of 2 and 3 are Earth and Wood respectively. Their Elements are incompatible and the second and third cycles are distant from the seventh cycle. Building B is oriented southeast and the numbers of the Essence of the Stars are 6 and 8. The sixth cycle spells the good fortune of the building in the past and the number 8 the good fortune of the coming cycle. Moreover, their Elements are compatible, thus, the building is well-oriented.

The Influences of the Jiuxing System on Selected Palaces

As the main palaces of the Forbidden City were built in AD 1420 during the eryun (second cycle) of the Jiuxing system their entrances were sited in the auspicious positions for this period.[28] However, the qi was exhausted by the time the yun was in the fifth cycle.[29] The Tai Hedian, the Zhong Hedian and the Bao Hedian were destroyed by fire in AD 1597. The Qian Qinggong and the Kun Minggong were constructed during the eryun era and their entrances were located in the qi areas. But in AD 1514 (during the yiyun period) they were destroyed by fire. Palaces built during the sanyun (third cycle) should not be oriented in the same direction as those built during the eryun (second cycle) and the qi of those built during the sanyun became more vibrant during the siyun (fourth cycle). Similarly, the yun of the fourth cycle changed during the fifth cycle.[30]

Architectural Planning and Detailing with Reference to Feng Shui

Palaces and buildings of grandeur were built by emperors of ancient times as early as the Shang dynasty (1711–1066 BC). According to classical records it was reported that the scale of the palaces was quite impressive and some measured 80 metres

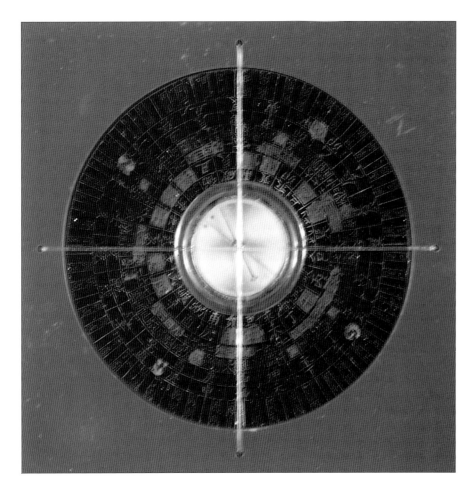

A thousand years ago the Chinese started to make complicated compasses based on the theory of the *Yijing,* the philosophy of *yin* and *yang* and the theory of the Five Elements. This ancient *luopan* is a special compass based on these theories.

During the third century BC the Chinese were making magnetic compasses named *sinan* which took the form of a spoon on a bronze earth-plate. In this Han dynasty *luopan* the handle of the spoon would always point south.

long and 15 metres wide. Building construction techniques and skills improved and by the Qin 秦 dynasty the standard of workmanship improved and the scale of the structures increased. For example, the Qin Xianyang 秦咸阳 palace complex built during the Qin era consisted of several blocks of impressive buildings. During the Han dynasty the palace complex and city, Changan were sizeable in scale. During the Tang period in Changan 长安 the palace, Da Minggong 大明宫, was constructed on a grand scale with refined detailing. By the Ming and Qing dynasties the techniques and skill of construction reached the peak. Based on balance, symmetry and harmony the planning, scale and grandeur of the imperial palaces was outstanding. The detailing of the palaces was superbly executed. Every detail of the roof, the elevation, the section and structural elements was designed with reference to the precepts of *feng shui*, and every decorative element was symbolically auspicious.

The Feng Shui of Palace Names

Most of the names of the imperial palaces were derived from words in the *Si Shu* 四书 (ancient Classics namely *Da Xue* 大学, *Zhong Yong* 中庸, *Lun Yu* 论语 and *Mengzi* 孟子) and the *Wujing* 五经 (Confucian Classics namely *Shijing* 诗经, *Shujing* 书经, *Liji* 礼记, *Yijing* 易经 and *Chunqiu* 春秋). The most important of the Gugong palaces are the Tai Hedian, the Zhong Hedian and the Bao Hedian. Their names were picked from auspicious and meaningful words in the *Yijing*, the Book of Changes, possibly for *feng shui* reasons. It was believed that the words 'Tai He' implied the harmony of *yin* and *yang* forces. In the Qian 乾 Xiangci 象辞 of the *Yijing* the words 'Bao He' and 'Tai He' are auspicious words that imply harmony between nature and man and between the ruler and his people. The words 'Zhong He' are found in the *Liji*, the Confucian Classics, and imply that on earth all things will grow, all men will feel contented and all will enjoy peace and harmony. Even the names of residential palaces such as the Qian Qinggong, the Kun Ninggong and the Jiao Taidian were taken from the *Yijing*. The names refer to the harmony of the natural and cosmological forces. However, the Elements of the individual words had not been carefully considered. 'Tai' is Fire and 'He' Water; therefore Tai Hedian would not be considered auspicious because the Fire Element of the word 'Tai' would clash with the Water Element of 'He'. Tai Hedian burnt down several times after its completion.[31]

Application of Yin, Yang, Colours and the Five Elements

The planning of the Gugong is based on the precepts of *feng shui* 风水, the art of placement with reference to a sense of balance, the theory of *yin* and *yang*, the orientation of the sun, the direction of wind and the flow of water courses.[32] To the north of the Gugong is the Tai Hengshan and to the east is the Bohai 勃海. The water stream from the man-made Beihai comes from the *qian* (northwest) direction and flows out to the *sun* (southeast) direction according to the theory of *feng shui*. The stream that comes from the west is named the Jin Shuihe 金水河 (Golden Water Stream – gold is associated with the west). The entire city is planned on an axial line to achieve balance and symmetry. The hierarchy, order and formality of spaces within the palatial complex were based on the order and system stated in the *Liji* 礼记 and *Kao Gongji* 考工记.[33] The city is sited to face south which was considered an auspicious direction coinciding with the direction associated with the emperor.[34] The city is symbolically divided into four parts – the east, south, west and north. The east which is associated with the Wood Element, the sun and the springtime is classified as *yang*. Qing dynasty palaces positioned in the east were for those born in the year of the Wood Element. The south which is the Fire Element, the hot sun and

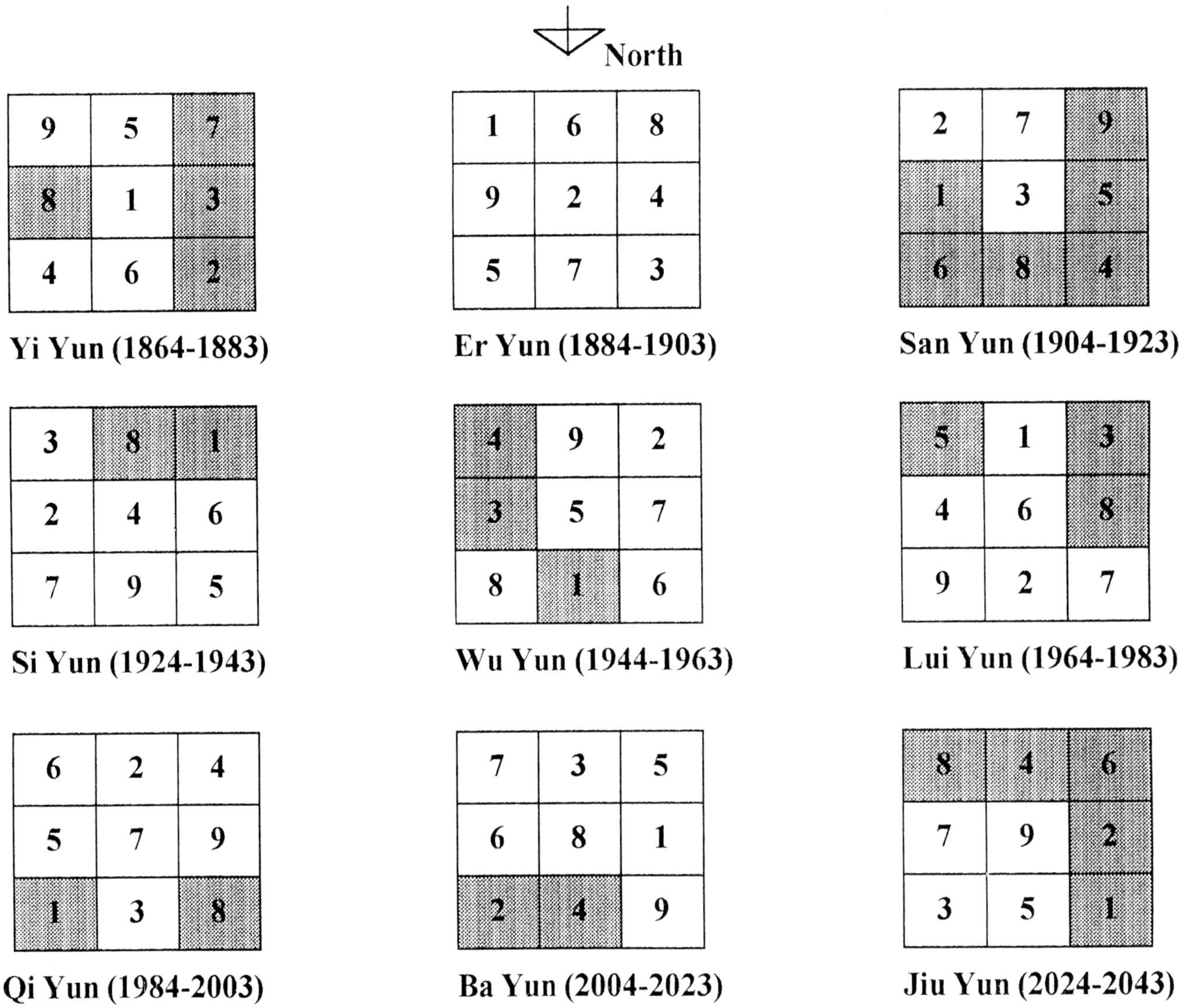

9	5	7
8	1	3
4	6	2

Yi Yun (1864-1883)

1	6	8
9	2	4
5	7	3

Er Yun (1884-1903)

2	7	9
1	3	5
6	8	4

San Yun (1904-1923)

3	8	1
2	4	6
7	9	5

Si Yun (1924-1943)

4	9	2
3	5	7
8	1	6

Wu Yun (1944-1963)

5	1	3
4	6	8
9	2	7

Lui Yun (1964-1983)

6	2	4
5	7	9
1	3	8

Qi Yun (1984-2003)

7	3	5
6	8	1
2	4	9

Ba Yun (2004-2023)

8	4	6
7	9	2
3	5	1

Jiu Yun (2024-2043)

Diagrams of the Jiuxing illustrate the magic diagrams of *yun* (lucky and unlucky spells) of various door openings with reference to the orientations. The grey areas are inauspicious for entrance doors.

This simple *luopan* gives readings of directions with reference to the Ten Stems and Twelve Branches.

summer time is supreme *yang*. Tai Hedian is positioned to face south. The west which is associated with the Gold Element, sunset and autumn is *yin*. Palaces for the empress and concubines were thus sited in the west. The north is the Water Element and winter and is *yin*. The Coal Hill is used to reduce the *yinqi* or negative energy.

The main palaces are built to face south, away from a man-made hill built up of coal and the earth dug out of the Tong Zihe, which symbolises the solid backing at the rear of the site of the palaces. A man-made lake brings water from the north which then flows from the lake to surround the palace compound and passes the main gateways.[35] This water course, called the Golden Water Stream, symbolises 'wealth flowing into the royal household'.[36]

Everything in the Zi Jincheng, be it in its natural or man-made form, is supposed to be balanced with reference to its nature (*yin* and *yang*) and its element. The structures in the Gugong are classified either *yin* or *yang*. For example, the buildings used as public administration areas are *yang* while the private or residential quarters are *yin*. The front facades are *yang* while the rear *yin*. The roof tops are *yang* and the roof eaves *yin*. The sunlit courts are *yang* and the shaded corridors *yin*. The red columns are *yang* and the green ceilings *yin*. The tiers of steps with odd numbers are *yang* and those with even numbers *yin*. Three (an odd number) main public palaces must be contrasted with two (an even number) residential palaces. Thus the palace complex is divided into *waichao* 外朝 (*yang*) and *neiting* 内亭 (*yin*). *Waichao* consists of palaces for public administration and *neiting* for private residence. The *yang* public areas are built in numbers of *yang* right down to finishing or paving materials. The private halls are *yin* in terms of building blocks and finishing materials. The Tai Hedian is the supreme *yang* building and its facades are designed in eleven bays by five bays (both 11 and 5 are *yang* numbers). The Qian Qinggong, built as the emperor's residence and based on the *qian* 乾 trigram also has a nine-bay facade. Within each palace the side facing the sun (*yang*) is finished with *yang* coloured materials and the side facing north (*yin*) is paved with *yin* coloured materials. For example, the front podium of Qian Qinggong has white (*yang*) marble balustrades while its north side has a green (*yin*) podium.

Every family member of the Qing emperor was allocated his or her residential palace according to his or her horoscope or element of birth. The Wen Huadian 文华殿 was built for the crown prince of emperor Qian Long because he was of Wood Element and his palace had to be positioned at the east side and be covered with a green roof. The emperor's favourite concubine, Taifei 太妃, was of Gold Element and her residence had to be positioned in the west. Garden walls were painted according to where they were positioned. Those in the east were painted green, those in the south red, those in the west white, those in the north black and those in the centre yellow. Wen Yuange was covered with black tiles because black (Water Element) was believed to have control over fire. Nan Sansuo, once used by the prince as his residence, is covered with green tiles to signify longevity.

The Application of Numerology

The number 9 which signifies the highest order of the *yang* quality has been used repeatedly on the structures of the Gugong. As mentioned earlier the total number of rooms in the Gugong was nine thousand nine hundred and ninety-nine.[37] The Tai Hemen is also known as Jiuji Gongmen 九脊宫门 (Imperial Gate with Nine Roof Ridges). The roof of the Tai Hedian is also called Jiuji Fengshilong 九脊封十龙 (Nine Ridges with Ten Dragons). This demonstrates that the number 9 is considered a powerful number worthy of representing the imperial power. It has also been repeatedly used on the Tiantan for paving patterns.

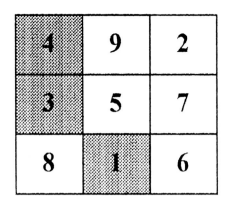

This diagram of the fifth cycle and *yun* of the imperial palaces shows that the orientations of the main palaces were auspicious when they were first built but when the cycle of *yun* changed with time, the *feng shui* of the palaces was also affected adversely.

Even the doors of the palaces in the Gugong are designed with *feng shui* numbers in mind. Some of the doors are detailed in such a way that they have rows of *mending* 门钉 (metal ornaments on the doors) and the number of *mending* varies from three to nine in a horizontal or vertical row. The main doors are *yang* doors and therefore have nine horizontally and nine vertically, making the total eighty-one (an auspicious number, 8 being *yin* and 1 being *yang*).[38]

During imperial rule the number 9 was associated with the emperor whose subjects had to greet him with 'san gui jiu kou' 三跪九叩 (kneel three times and knock the head on the ground nine times). The numerical 9 was applied to units of construction and to bays of building. Presents for the royal household were made in pairs of nine. For example, on the sixtieth birthday of empress dowager, Cixi, the top government officials presented nine boxes of *ruyi* 如意 (precious jade), each box containing nine pieces of jade making the total eighty-one, for auspicious significance.

Feng Shui Elements in the Roofs of the Gugong

The ridges of the roofs of the buildings in the Gugong were constructed with many elements that augur auspicious significance and *feng shui* elements. The *feilong* 飞龙 (dancing dragons) flanking the pearl represent the perfect balance of *yin* and *yang*. The fish signifies success, the elephant wisdom, the phoenix beauty and *yin* power, the horse vitality, the lion strength, and the *chi* 蚩 or fish dragon the power to bring rain during a dry season and to deter fire hazards. Sometimes a sword is placed at the tail of the *chi* to stop it escaping. During the Ming dynasty the *chi* was called *wenshou* 吻兽 (kissing animal). There are various types of *wen*. The ones on the ends of the main ridge are called *zhengwen* 正文. Those on the roof corner ribs are named *chuishou* 垂兽. The more important a building is the more roof animal ornaments it has. However, the maximum number does not exceed eleven and even the most important building in the Gugong, the Tai Hedian, has only nine roof animal ornaments on each roof corner rib.[39]

Many wells were dug in the Zi Jincheng, some of which are covered by pavilions that have small openings on the roofs. These roof openings are *feng shui* elements because without them the water is said to be 'shui bude yangguang shi chunyin zhishui' 水不得阳光是纯阴之水 (water without the sun's rays is pure *yin* water). *Yin* water is not good for the health and so it must be turned into *yang*.

The Design of Other Elements with Reference to Feng Shui

The imperial seat on the throne of the Tai Hedian was also designed with the most auspicious symbols. It contains nine dragons incorporated in the design and the seat was named *jiulong baozuo* 九龙宝座 (precious seat with nine dragons).

When the Zi Jincheng was built there were as many as three hundred and eight water vessels which were made of steel or bronze. The eighteen in front of the Tai Hedian were gilded. These vessels, named *menhai* 门海 (doors of sea), were *feng shui* elements and contained water for fire fighting. It was believed that water (symbolic of the sea) placed in front of the doors would bring good luck. Since there was no specific fire-fighting equipment at that time the huge containers were most appropriate for holding water for fighting a fire. During winter months when the water turned into ice the vessels were heated underneath to maintain the water in its liquid state.[40]

The main doors of the palaces in the Gugong were designed with reference to *feng shui* and each had to coincide with the Lubanche or *feng shui* ruler.[41] The palaces in the Gugong were raised on podiums. All imperial palaces used by the emperor had to be 9 feet high (Chinese ruler) as nine signified the supreme *yang*.[42]

The design of the four corner towers of the wall enclosure also accorded with *feng shui* reasons. The entire palace complex faces south which is *qian*, the supreme *yang* according to the Former Heaven Trigram Arrangement.[43] But the corners which are off the cardinal points are considered less auspicious, and therefore, the towers are placed at the corners to neutralise any ill-effects. The elaborate design of the towers is also to accentuate the important part they play in the entire design.

The *feng shui* symbolism of some of the building structures is as shown in the chart below.

Structure	Symbolism
East Gate	Sun
West Gate	Moon
East and West Palaces	Twelve Hours of the Day
East and West Lodges	Five Elements
Administration in the south	*Yang*
Residential in the north	*Yin*
Tai Hedian	The *Yang* of *Yang*
Zhong Hedian	The balance of *Yin* and *Yang*
Bao Hedian	The *Yang* of *Yin*
Qian Qinggong	The *Yin* of *Yang*
Kun Ninggong	The *Yin* of *Yin*

綺望樓

The Coal Hill, a man-made hill, is situated behind the northern
gate, the Shen Wumen. The Jingshan was constructed from coal
and earth. It is 46 metres high and has five peaks covered with
pine trees and plants. From here the entire roofscape of the
Forbidden City can be seen.

Notes

1 See Needham, Joseph, *Science and Civilisation in China*, Cambridge University Press (Cambridge) Vol 2, 1956. See Eitel, Ernest, *Feng Shui or the Rudiments of Natural Science in China*, Lane Crawford (Hong Kong) 1973. Other writers considered *feng shui* a unique science of site planning. Also see Anderson, Eugene and Marja, *Mountains and Water: Essays on the Cultural Ecology of South Coastal China*, Orient Cultural Services (Taipei) 1973, pp49-50.

2 See Lip, Evelyn, *Out of China, Culture and Traditions*, Addison-Wesley (Singapore, New York) 1993, pp55-69.

3 See *Out of China*, ibid, p62.

4 The ancient theory of *feng shui* includes the Leshu 洛书 diagrams of *qi* locations with reference to the orientations of buildings and the nine cycles of *yuan* 元 (*feng shui* periods), each of twenty years making a total of one hundred and eighty years. For example, the first cycle started in 1684 and ended in 1703; the second was from 1704 to 1723; the third from 1724 to 1743; the fourth from 1744 to 1763; the fifth from 1764 to 1783; the sixth from 1784 to 1803; the seventh from 1804 to 1823; the eighth from 1824 to 1843; and the ninth from 1844 to 1863. The next one hundred and eighty year cycle started again in 1864 and will end in 2043.

5 The process of weathering on the sites of buildings can also be referred to as a part of *dili* 地理 (geography).

6 Therefore, the *feng shui* of a country could be affected by the political situation and vice versa.

7 See Lip, Evelyn, *Chinese Geomancy*, Times Editions (Singapore) 1979. Also see illustrations on pp72, 96 for examples of buildings that were built with artificial features to enhance the *feng shui* of the sites.

8 The hill at the rear of a building is named *leshan* 乐山 and preferably it should have a well-defined profile. Ideally, further away from the *leshan* hills there should be a range of hills which the *kanyu* expert named *longmai* 龙脉 (pulse of the dragon). On the left and right sides of the site there should be higher ground.

9 The *Lushi Chunqiu* states that what happens on earth is related to the cosmological influence. *Huainanzi* was written by Huai Nanhuang and his associates in the west Han era. It is Taoist in essence and discusses the *yin* and *yang* theory. The *Guanzi* was edited by Guan Zhong of the Chunqiu era and discusses the cosmological, geographical and many other natural and economic influences on man. Other classical writings dating back to the Zhou dynasty that contained evidences of choosing auspicious sites for new capitals were the *Shujing* (the Book of Documents) and the *Shijing* (the Book of Songs).

10 See Lip, Evelyn, *Out of China, Culture and Traditions*, op cit, p78. Also see Lip, Evelyn, *Chinese Temples and Deities*, Times Books International (Singapore) 1986, p9.

11 *Feng shui* was not just applied to living quarters. Emperors of the Five Dynasties and later dynasties were buried in tombs on hilly sites.

12 *Liqi* or energy of the earth is also influenced by the cosmic *qi*. For example, extremely heavy and continuous rainfall may cause landslides and destroy the energy of the earth.

13 See Lip, Evelyn, *Chinese Geomancy*, ibid, p29 and see Lip, Evelyn, *Out of China*, ibid, pp63-65. The Nine Stars are *Tanlang* 贪狼 (Wood Element, auspicious), *Jumen* 巨门 (Earth, auspicious), *Lucun* 禄存 (Earth), *Wenqu* 文曲 (Water, inauspicious), *Lianzhen* 廉贞 (Fire, inauspicious), *Wuqu* 武曲 (Gold, auspicious), *Pojun* 破军 (Gold, inauspicious), *Zuofu* 左辅 (Earth inauspicious) and *Youbi* 右弼 (Water, uncertain). From the orientation of the building the Element is obtained, and from the association of the Nine Stars with the Elements the auspiciousness of the building can be assessed.

14 See Lip, Evelyn, *Feng Shui For The Home*, Times Books International (Singapore) 1986, pp26-30. Charts are given in this book to assist the assessment of a building. Also see Lip, Evelyn, *Feng Shui For Business*, Times Books International (Singapore) 1989, pp33-38.

15 The Trigrams are: *qian* 乾, *kun* 坤, *chen* 辰, *kan* 坎, *gen* 艮, *xun* 巽, *li* 离, and *dui* 兑. *Qian*, indicated by three solid lines, refers to the heavens, the sun, masculinity and the northwest. *Kun*, represented by three broken lines, refers to the earth, the moon, femininity, and the southwest. *Chen*, symbolised by two broken lines and a solid line, represents change in things and the east direction. *Kan*, represented by a solid line sandwiched by two broken lines, means danger; it refers to the north direction. *Gen*, represented by a solid and two broken lines, symbolises obstacle and it refers to the northeast. *Xun*, shown as two solid lines and one broken line, is equated to influence and the southeast. *Li*, denoted by a broken line sandwiched by two solid lines, means firmness and the south direction. *Dui*, indicated by one broken and two solid lines, means happiness and the west direction.

16 See Feng Yulan, *A History of Chinese Philosophy*, Princeton University Press (Princeton) 1953, Vol 2 p8 note 3.

17 Another legendary leader called Yu saw the Trigrams on the back of a huge tortoise on the Le River during the time of the great floods. The arrangement of the trigrams was later interpreted by Wen Wang (1231-1135 BC), the first emperor of the Zhou dynasty, in a cyclical formation from *qian* 乾, *kan* 坎, *gen* 艮, *chen* 辰, *xun* 巽, *li* 离, *kun* 坤 to *dui* 兑. See Lip, Evelyn, *Out of China*, op cit, p58.

18 Lao Zi 老子, the ancient sage and founder of Taoism, said that the formation and changes of things were the result of the fusion of *yin* and *yang* ingredients.

19 It is expressed in the *Lushi Chunqiu* that buildings that are imbalanced in *yin*, *yang* and the Elements are not habitable because of the unseen inauspicious influence on the tenants.

20 The orientation of a site is referred to by the Nine Stars but the land form is referred to by the planets. See Needham, Joseph, op cit, Vol 3 p250.

21 See Lip, Evelyn, *Out of China*, op cit, p60. Also see Jean-Michel Huon de Kermadec (translated by Poulsen, Derek), *The Way to Chinese Astrology, The Four Pillars of Destiny*, Unwin Paperbacks (London) 1986, pp82-83. Among other sources, the *Shujing* provides a Chinese system of correlations of the Five Elements with the directions, the colours, the planets and the relationship of the elements with each other.

22 See illustration on p72 for an example of buildings with man-made hills built behind for the enhancement of *feng shui*.

23 One cycle is named *nian* and each *nian* is made up of three hundred and sixty-five days. Each year is associated with an animal symbol. For example, from 2 February 1984 to 19 February 1985 was the *Jaizi* 甲子 *nian* and year of the Rat. The years that follow are: *Yichou* 乙丑 (Ox); *Bingyin* 丙寅 (Tiger); *Dingmao* 丁卯 (Rabbit); *Wuchen* 戊辰 (Dragon); *Jisi* 已巳 (Snake); *Gengwu* 庚午 (Horse); *Xinwei* 辛未 (Goat); *Renshen* 壬申 (Monkey); *Guiyou* 癸酉 (Rooster); *Jiashu* 甲戌 (Dog) and *Yihai* 乙亥 (Pig). Also see Lip, Evelyn, *Fun With Chinese Horoscopes*, Graham Brash (Singapore) 1981.

24 The Ten Heavenly Stems are: *Jia* 甲, *Yi* 乙, *Bing* 丙, *Ding* 丁, *Wu* 戊, *Ji* 己, *Geng* 庚, *Xin* 辛, *Ren* 壬 and *Kui* 癸. The Twelve Earthly Branches are: *Zi* 子, *Chou* 丑, *Yin* 寅, *Mao* 卯, *Chen* 辰, *Si* 巳, *Wu* 午, *Wei* 未, *Shen* 申, *You* 酉, *Shu* 戌 and *Hai* 亥.

25 Both *Lushi Chunqiu* and *Huainanzi* have records of the cyclical changes of the seasons.

26 Good *qi* prevails when an auspicious time is chosen for an activity. This was illustrated in the *Huangdi Zhaijing* 黄帝宅经 Vol 1 p16.

27 The Essence of the Stars was first discovered by Fuxi, the first legendary emperor of China. It appears that the influences of the dragon veins or *qi* change with time and space. The Leshu diagrams as shown on p68 show the changes from the first to the ninth cycle, each cycle spanning over a twenty-year period.

28 See diagram on p68. From the Leshu magic diagram the main entrances of the palaces were located at the prosperous double 2. It is understood that number 2 takes precedence during the *eryun* (second cycle) while 3 spells great fortune during the third cycle.

29 See diagram on p70 for the Leshu diagram of the fifth cycle. The number 2 Essence of the Star is auspicious for a building constructed during the *eryun* (second cycle) and the number 3 is significant as it spells the prosperity of the immediate future. But the numbers 1,9, 8, 7, 6, 5, or even 4 are not auspicious as the prosperity they bring is rather in the distant future. When the two numbers in the square are read their Elements must be compatible. Since 1 is Water, 2 is Earth, 3 is Wood, 4 is Wood, 5 is Earth, 6 is Gold, 7 is Gold, 8 is Earth and 9 is Fire. The auspicious combinations are: 1 and 3, 1 and 4, 2 and 6, 2 and 7, 3 and 9, 4 and 9, 5 and 6, 5 and 7, 6 and 1, 7 and 1, 8 and 6, 8 and 7, 9 and 2, 9 and 5, and 9 and 8. The inauspicious numbers are: 1 and 9, 2 and 1, 3 and 2, 3 and 5, 3 and 8, 4 and 2, 4 and 5, 4 and 8, 5 and 1, 6 and 3, 6 and 4, 7 and 4, 8 and 1, 9 and 6, and 9 and 7.

30 See the Leshu diagrams on pp68, 70. Note the diagram of the *eryun* spells auspiciousness for all directions of entry. By the time the *sanyun* takes place the main entrance of the building oriented to face south has become inauspicious. The same building has its luck changed by the fourth cycle. However, the *qi* of the main entrance becomes exhausted by the fifth cycle. Therefore, it is understood that the cycles of *feng shui* change over time and space and the siting of buildings has to be considered with reference to the 'birth' date of the building.

31 See Lip, Evelyn, *Choosing Auspicious Chinese Names*, Times Books International (Singapore) 1988, p13. The auspiciousness of a Chinese name is assessed by the following: the Elements or sound of the words in the name; the *yin*, *yang* or total number of strokes in the name; the meaning; and the horoscope. A person's date of birth is also considered in the assessment. Also see the diagram on p70 which shows the inauspiciousness of the date the Tai Hedian burnt down.

32 See Lip, Evelyn, *Feng Shui For Business*, op cit, p21.

33 The *Liji* was a Classic edited by Confucius (sixth century BC) elaborating on the etiquette and systems of the ancient society. The *Kao Gongji* was first written during the Qin dynasty (third century BC) and in the Chunqiu era (eighth-sixth century BC) it was re-edited to contain the techniques of building construction.

34 South is symbolic of the Fire Element and it is *yang* in nature. The emperor being the symbol of supreme *yang* is associated with the south.

35 Water symbolises wealth and it is made to pass the main gate or door to signify that wealth comes to the household.

36 See Lip, Evelyn, *Out of China, Culture and Traditions*, Addison-Wesley (Singapore) 1993, p60. The Chinese believe that the workings of the Five Elements (Gold, Wood, Water, Fire and Earth) are seen in nature. All things in the physical world can be classified under the Five Elements. The Elements react with each other either in a productive or destructive manner. The Water Element associated with north, should come from this direction. Ponds, lakes, water features and fountains of buildings should be located to the north or northern parts of sites.

37 In this case the lower floor of the Wen Yuange which contains only a staircase is not counted as one building.

38 The exceptional case is found on the door of Dong Huamen which has seventy-two metal ornaments (eight by nine). But seventy-two was not its original number. When it was first constructed it had eighty-one (nine by nine) but when Li Zhicheng led the rebels to Beijing the Ming emperor left the Zi Jincheng through

the Dong Huamen and retreated to the Coal Hill where he hanged himself. During the Qing rule one row of the metal ornaments were taken out to improve the *feng shui* of the door.

39 See pp57, 60 for examples of roofs with ornaments as described. The palaces used by the emperor were decorated with nine ornaments to show supreme *yang*.

40 Wang Daren 王达人 and Wang Dianying 王殿英, *Gugong Daguang* 故宫大观, Chongqing Chuban She 重庆出版社, (Chongqing) 1987, p32.

41 The ruler is divided into eight parts. The first indicates *cai* 财 (prosperity), the second *bing* 病 (sickness), the third *li* 离 (separation), the fourth *yi* 义 (righteousness), the fifth *guan* 官 (official), the sixth *jie* 劫 (robbed), the seventh *hai* 害 (harm) and the eighth *ben* 本 (origin). The measurement of all main doors should be checked with the ruler to ensure that they are auspicious. See Lip, Evelyn, *Chinese Geomancy*, op cit, p39.

42 Podiums of buildings for top officials were 7 feet high, for top scholars 5 feet, and for ordinary men up to 3 feet.

43 The Former Heaven Trigrams Arrangement is related to the Hetu which consists of fifty-five dots of *yin* and *yang*. It is believed that the Hetu represents the source of heavenly principles.

Chinese Temples

In China, temples are classified by scholars and historians according to their religious denomination and they fall into into five categories; *si* 寺, *gong* 宫, *miao* 庙, *ci* 祠 and *an* 庵.[1] *Si* are usually the largest temples and are generally Buddhist.[2] *Miao* temples are most frequently larger than *gong* but smaller than *si*, and are often used for offering sacrifices to the ancestors or for the worship of Syncretic deities. *Gong* are usually the third largest and are often used by Taoists.[3] *Ci* are for paying respect to ancestors or to Confucius. *An* are nunneries for female Buddhist vegetarians.

Other names for temples are: *tang* 堂, *ting* 亭, *dian* 殿, *yuan* 院, *ge* 阁, and *tan* 坛.[4] Some temples bear the name of the principal deity worshipped. For example, Guan Yinge is for the worship of Guan Yin, the Goddess of Mercy.

Religious Deities

The Chinese people have many beliefs. Their ancestors worship a great number of gods and many natural elements and phenomena – the moon, the sun, the stars, thunder, lightning and animals such as the tiger, the unicorn and other mythical animals. Generally, deities can be classified according to their religious denomination.

Buddhist deities include Shakyamuni Buddha, Amitabha, Maitreya Buddha, Kshitgarbha Buddha, Ananda and the Buddha's other disciples, Cheng Huang or City God, the Diamond Kings and the Goddess of Mercy. Taoist deities are the Yu Huang 玉皇, the Queen of Heavens, the Eight Immortals, the God of Literature, the God of Longevity, the God of Wealth, the God of Luck, Guan Di 关帝, the Monkey God, the Kitchen God and many others such as the Bao Sheng Dadi 宝生大帝 and the Qing Shui Zushi 清水祖师. In a Confucian temple Confucius is the main figure. In temples for ancestor worship, spirit tablets of the ancestors and a deity associated with clan legends or a historical figure are honoured. Temples dedicated to denominations other than the above may include those that are built for the practice of the Three-in-One or Doctrine of the Great Way of the Former Heaven. In such a temple legendary figures and Taoist deities may be worshipped. Thus, it is important to note the main deities worshipped in order to classify the temple; when the main deities are Buddhist the temple is Buddhist.

Temple Architecture

Buddhism was brought into China as early as the Han dynasty. By the Northern Wei period twelve thousand seven hundred temples were built.[5] In terms of concept the planning of a temple is not different from that of a palace or house depending on the scale and importance of the temple.[6] The concept of planning of the imperial palace complex in the Forbidden City is similar to that of a large temple complex. The plan is based upon symmetry and the courtyard concept. Indeed, during the Qing dynasty a palace could be converted into a temple, as exemplified by the changing of the palace of emperor Yong Zheng 雍正 into a temple which was named Yong Hegong 雍和宫. The concept based on the *si heyuan* 四合院 (four blocks forming a garden)

Gateway of the Huanqiu

was adopted for temple building as early as the Han dynasty. The size of the temple was determined by its importance – the more important the temple the more courtyards it contained.

The structural system of a temple also follows that of a residential or palatial building. The typical beam-framed system is used for the support of the roof and other elements.[7] The roof forms may be classified under the hipped, the gabled, the half-hipped/half-gabled and the pyramid. The importance of a temple is reflected by the roof design. The more important the temple the more elaborate the roof. An important temple has a two- or three-tiered roof which can be half hipped/half-gabled.

All walls are screen walls rather than load bearing. In the north where the weather is severe the walls may be masonry and built very thick but in the south the walls are thinner and may even be built of timber. A large variety of shapes is employed for openings on the walls.[8]

Colour schemes of temples are based on traditional values of Chinese colours and the balance of *yin* (cool) and *yang* (warm) colours as shown in the chart below.

Colour	red	yellow	green	white	black
Element	Fire	Earth	Wood	Gold	Water
Nature	*yang*	*yang*	*yin*	*yang*	*yin*

Feng Shui for Temples

Reference is made to the precepts of geomancy and metaphysics when a temple is designed and constructed.[9] In the construction of the temple roof the roof ridge and its ornaments must be built correctly so that the balance of *yin* and *yang* forces are ensured and auspicious significance and heavenly blessings are bestowed upon the users. When the roof tiles are laid it is vital to start the laying of tiles from the centre of the roof and work towards the left and right sides rather than to start laying the tiles from one side to the other. There are two types of bamboo tiles commonly used: a half round tile and a shallow curved tile. It is important to start laying the shallow curved tiles at the centre of the roof first before laying any other line of tiles.

Auspicious dimensions and numerology must be applied by making reference to the geomantic ruler and Chinese symbolism. Odd numbers (*yang*) are good while even numbers (*yin*) are inauspicious. The shallow curved tiles of the roof at the centre must not be the eighth, eighteenth, twenty-eighth or thirty-eighth line of tiles counting from any sides or corners of the roof. Steps of staircases must also be odd in number to ensure the *yang* quality.

The orientation and siting of the temple is subject to all the rules spelt out in geomancy theory. Usually northeast or southwest directions are avoided as they are believed to be the doors for evil. Main doors are painted with images of the Door Gods or dragons and they are guarded by two (*yin* and *yang*) stone lions. The siting of a temple also depends on the surrounding environment and natural topography.[10] Where possible it is best to have hills behind and waterways in front.[11]

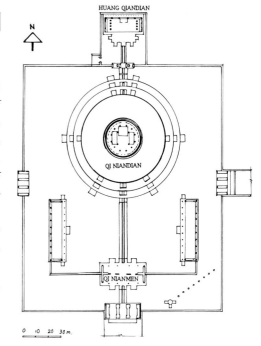

Tiantan 天坛, the Temple of Heaven

The temple complex of the Tiantan consists of three main structures namely Qi Niandian 祈年殿 (the Hall of Prayers for a Good Year), Zhaigong 斋宫 (the Hall of Abstinence) and Huanqiu 环丘 (the Circular Mound or the Altar of Heaven). The Tiantan is located just outside the inner city wall on an extensive park at the southeastern side of Beijing and enclosed by walls (measuring 1,700 by 1,600 metres). It served a special purpose during the Ming and Qing eras as it was the place of worship for the emperors. An auspicious day was chosen in the first lunar month for the emperor to pray at the Qi Niandian for good harvests throughout the year. In the fourth lunar month the emperor prayed for rain on the Huanqiu. On the day before the winter solstice, the emperor prepared himself for the worship of the heavens by fasting and meditating in the Zhaigong. He then proceeded to the Qi Niandian to pray for good harvesting for the nation. On the morning of the solstice, he would revisit the Zhaigong and then make offerings to the heavens on the Huanqiu.

The approach to the temple complex is imposing. Two entrances at the west lead to the inner area encircled by the high enclosing wall. Out of the two, one named Tan Ximen 坛西门 leads the way to the Xi Tianmen 西天门. The Zhaigong is first to be seen on the right. The Qi Niandian is seen in the north while the Huang Qiongyu 皇穹宇 and Huanqiu are seen in the south. The Qi Niandian, the Huang Qiongyu and the Yuanqiu are connected by a raised platform measuring 400 metres in length.

The 38-metre high Qi Niandian is built on a podium of three marble terraces, each tier is marked by a marble balustrade which has a base with cyma recta and cyma reversa mouldings. The plan of the Qi Niandian is round and it is covered with a three-tier circular roof of blue glazed tiles.[12] Blue symbolises heavenly blessings and the number 3 is a *yang* number to portray the emperor being a powerful and dynamic ruler.[13] The interior of the temple has three tiers of columns in two concentric circles. One circle has twelve columns, symbolising the twelve double hours and the other is made up of four central and twelve outer columns signifying the twelve months of the year.[14] The inner columns are gilded. Four inner 18-metre-high red columns, named Long Jinzhu 龙金柱, symbolise the four seasons of the year. The roof structure is ornately finished. The eaves' overhangs are supported by intricate brackets decorated with themes of phoenix and dragon representing the balance of *yin* and *yang* forces. The internal floor is 30 metres in diameter and 4 metres higher than the ground outside the temple, so that the temple floor level is almost 10 metres above ground level three terraces below.

The interior and ceiling of the Qi Niandian are lavishly ornate. The coffered ceiling is raised by tie beams elaborately painted in green and blue. The dome is raised by four tiers of brackets. The crown of the dome is gilded with the motif of the dancing phoenix and dragon. The floor is paved with flagstones and its centre finished with a marble slab, the natural veining of which resembles a phoenix dancing with a dragon. In the centre is a long antique table and a throne with a screen at its back. Two screens are placed at the east and an ornately carved birchwood screen is placed to the west. At the front are several precious antiques including a burner and a bronze tripod.

The southern group of buildings in the Tiantan comprises the Huang Qiongyu and the Huanqiu. The Huang Qiongyu is a small hall for the storage of ceremonial tablets or steles. It has a round, blue-glazed roof which is supported by eight eaves columns and eight *jinzhu* 金柱 (golden columns). Its concentric coffered ceiling is beautifully carved. The colour scheme is vivid, with a blue roof, red columns and window frames, and a white terrace.

The plan shows that the approach to the Qi Niandian through the Qi Nianmen is preceded by an entrance gateway. Both buildings are raised on podiums; the podium of Qi Niandian being circular in plan and constructed of white marble, has eight stairs, including the spirit ways on the central axis.

The Qi Niandian stands magnificently on its three-tier white marble podium and has a blue-glazed tile roof.

Internally the Qi Niandian is awe-inspiring and magnificent. Powerful *feng shui* and symbolism are expressed in the roof structure and decoration: circular roofs refer to the heavens and infinity; cloud motifs symbolise imperial power over the universe; and the *yang* images of dancing golden dragons and phoenix appear in sculptures and paintings on caissons and gold panels.

The gateway to the Huang Qiongyu and entry to the Hui Yingpi consists of three distinct arched entrances.

The Zhaigong is also round in plan. Its particular architectural features are the acoustics of the curved walls surrounding the courtyard. These walls are named Hui Yingpi 回音壁 and reflect sound so effectively that people standing on opposite sides can hear one another clearly. The stones paving the staircases also have special acoustics to reflect sound clearly.[15] During the Ming and Qing dynasties the emperors fasted in the Zhaigong on the day before the winter solstice.

The Huanqiu, south of the Qi Niandian, is modelled on an ancient sacrificial mound.[16] It was used by the emperor to worship the heavens. It is three-tiered and is constructed of masonry finished with white marble slabs. It can be approached from four directions. Each direction has a stair of nine steps, and all the marble paving slabs and balustrades are in numerals of nine (the *yang* number associated with the heavens).[17] The first and inner ring of the podium of the Huanqiu is paved with nine slabs, the second with eighteen and the third with twenty-seven. The ninth ring has eighty-one slabs.

Therefore, the three-tiered podium is paved with three thousand four hundred and two slabs. Every measurement and dimension is *yang* (or an odd number) because the mound was used by the emperor to worship the heavens. The flagstones on the terraces are arranged in nine concentric circles in multiples of nine. The innermost circle is made up of nine blocks of stone and the outermost eighty-one.

Indeed, the Tiantan is a unique piece of architecture built according to the advanced principles of mechanics and geometry available in the fifteenth century. The architectural detailing of both structural and non-structural elements is intricate and refined.

The elevational treatment of the facades and the colour scheme of the building elements are designed with reference to the harmony of the entire scheme. The subdivision of the wall panels into solid panels, latticework panels and doors is done taking into consideration the *yin* and *yang* in terms of numerology (3 and 4) and colour scheme (blue and red). The gold symbols of the ring beams and wall panels (*yang*) contrasts harmoniously with the blue (*yin*) background.

Surrounding the temple complex is a peaceful wooded area. Pine trees provide an effective backdrop to the complex which stands magnificently in the open space surrounding it.[18]

In summary, it can be said that the *feng shui* of the Tiantan is clearly expressed. The buildings and terraces of the Tiantan are round to symbolise the heavens. The entire setting and design (including the details) are based on *feng shui* precepts. For example, the number of paving slabs and the number of balusters on a terrace are *yang* (or an odd number) to signify the masculine power of the emperor. The three-tier terrace is also *yang* in symbolism.

The three-tier or triple conical roof of the Qi Niandian signifies *yang*. The roof colour is blue symbolising the heavens. The *baoding* gives a powerful termination to the glazed tiled round roof. The significance of the interior is illustrated by the coffered ceiling with auspicious *yin* and *yang* symbols such as phoenix and coiled dragons.

It is evident that the symbols used, the spatial effects created and the architectural theme as well as the structural composition of the Tiantan were significantly and intentionally created, the obvious reason being that the Tiantan was built for the emperor to offer sacrifices and prayers to the heavens and his ancestors. As the emperor was seen as the son of the heavens and possessing divine powers, his place of worship must be of the grandest scale and finished with the most ornate decorations. Offerings must furthermore be made in the most solemn of rituals in the most powerful environment.

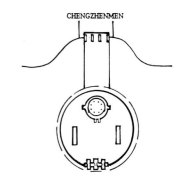

Other Temples in North China
Wo Fosi 卧佛寺

Situated west of Beijing is the Wo Fosi which was built AD 67 in the Tang dynasty. It is named and dedicated after the huge bronze sleeping Buddha which it houses. Its entry is through an impressive masonry gateway with three brick archways painted red and framed with white marble with protruding circular motifs depicting *mending* 门钉. The archway is terminated with glazed tiled roofs and ornamented with green and yellow glazed tiles and glazed panels with dragon motifs. Beyond this gateway is a pond of lilies crossed by a bridge which leads to the prayer halls.

The main prayer hall, the Tian Wangdian 天王殿, is covered with green and yellow glazed tiles. Its main ridge is terminated with yellow glazed *wenshou* 吻兽. The wall panels are elaborate and beautifully designed. The fourth hall houses the sleeping Buddha and twelve statues of Bodhisattvas.

Beyond the Buddha hall are five halls for the storage of sutras. In the courtyards of the temple complex are pavilions and an interesting variety of landscape elements.

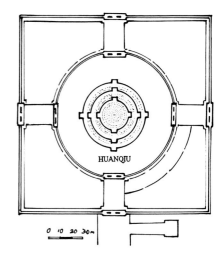

Bi Yunsi 碧云寺

Also situated to the west of Beijing is the Bi Yunsi which was originally built in the Yuan dynasty, and later rebuilt in the Ming period. The entire site is enhanced by the woods, hills and ponds around it. Water is brought from the springs in the hills to the ponds to give the temple a setting of serenity and beauty.

The architecture of this temple bears Indian and Lamaist influences as demonstrated by its pagodas and roof spires. The Jingang Baozuo 金刚宝 pagoda is modelled on Indian stupa design. Although its gateways are stone they were made to look like timber structures with bas-relief carvings of dragons and pearl motifs.

Circular in plan, the Huanqiu and Huang Qiongyu were both used by the emperors for the worship of the heavens. Approached from the Cheng Zhenmen in the north, the Huang Qiongyu was used to house the spirit tablets of the imperial rulers' ancestors.

Yong Hegong 雍和宫

The Yong Hegong is situated to the northeast of the eastern part of the city. Built in AD 1694 as the residence of prince Yong Zheng 雍正 it was converted, when he ascended the throne in AD 1744, into a Lamaist temple, which at its religious peak housed nine hundred monks. Entered through the *shanmen*, the first hall is the Yong Zhenmen which houses the Maitreya Buddha and the four Diamond Kings. The temple complex has a series of courtyards. The Yong Hegong is followed by the Fa Lundian 法轮殿 and the Wan Foge 万佛阁. The main hall, the Yong Hegong, is ornately built, complete with a colourful coffered ceiling. The importance of this hall is marked by the elaborate details of the roof, the *dougong* and the structural, as well as non-structural, elements. Each of the roof corner ribs is decorated with seven mythical ceramic animals. The hall houses three statues of the Buddha and the Eighteen Arhats. Beyond this is the hall for the worship of Buddha. Beyond the Buddha hall is the Fa Lundian 法轮殿 which is shaped like a cross. Its roof has five lantern and stupa-like structures on the ridge. This hall is for the worship of the most respected Lamaist monk and for the storage of sutras. Finally the most imposing 24-metre-high hall, the Wan Foge 万佛阁 is reached. Here the awe-inspiring 8-metre-tall statue of a Lamaist Buddha stands majestically in the hall. It was carved out of a single trunk of *zitan* (rosewood). Linked to the Wan Foge at the upper levels are the Yong Kangge (on the left) and the Yan Luange (on the right). These are very well built and detailed traditional buildings with ornate decorations.

The square three-tiered podium of the Qi Niandian is prominently defined. The roof apex is terminated with a *baoding* portraying celestial power. The bright red intricate latticework window and door panels are made by skilled craftsmen.

This detail of beams and column in the Qi Niandian shows the column supporting the beam. The colours of the interior structural members are vivid and brilliant.

Bai Yunguan 白云观

The Bai Yunguan is Beijing's largest Taoist temple. It was built as early as AD 739. Its name was changed many times (Tian Changguan 天长观 during the Tang dynasty and Tai Jigong 太极宫 during the Jin dynasty) before it was finally named Bai Yunguan. It was also rebuilt a few times over its long historical past, most recently during the Qing dynasty. Its main structures including the entrance gates, the Ling Guandian 灵官殿, the Yu Huangdian 玉皇殿 are on its axial line. The ancestor worship hall, the hall for the storage of sutras and residential halls form the innermost courtyard.

Fa Yuansi 法源寺

Beijing's oldest temple, the Fa Yuansi was constructed between AD 645–696. Its original name, Shun Tiansi 顺天寺, was replaced several times and it was not given its present name until AD 1734. It has six courtyards and consists of several important structures such as the main gateway, the drum and bell towers, the Tian Wangdian 天王殿, the Daxiong Baodian 大雄宝殿 and the Chang Jinglou 藏经搂.

Fo Xiangge 佛香阁

This building is situated on the hill slope of the Wan Shoushan 万寿山 in the Yi Heyuan, along the central axis of the complex. Built in AD 1736 it was destroyed in 1860, but later rebuilt by Guang Xu and reinstated to its original state. It has an octagonal plan covered by a three-tier roof. The four main hardwood columns are 30 metres in height.

Fa Mingsi 法明寺

The Fa Mingsi is situated in the east of the city and built in AD 1356 in a large compound of over 10,000 square metres. Its traditional classical architecture is magnificent and it houses the ancient sutras and valuable antiques.

Ba Dachu 八大处 Temple Complex

The Ba Dachu consists of eight well-known temples: the Chang Ansi 长安寺, the Ling Guangsi 灵光寺, the San Shanan 三山庵, the Da Beisi 大悲寺, the Long Wangtang 龙王堂, the Xiang Jiesi 香阶寺, the Bao Zhudong 宝珠洞 and the Mi Moyan 秘魔岩. These temples are located on the hills of Xishan 西山 Donglu 东麓 and Cui Weishan 翠微山. They are north of the river Yong Ding 永定, and south of the hills of Lu Shishan 庐师山. With level grassland in front, pine tree-covered hills behind and streams flowing past, the *feng shui* and landscape are ideal for the location of the temples. Three temples, the Chang Ansi, the San Shanan and Ling Guangsi are sited at the foot of the hills, the Da Beisi, Long Wangtang and Xiang Jiesi are sited on the slopes of the hills while the Bao Zhudong and Zheng Guosi are on the tops of the hills.

The Chang Ansi was built in AD 1504. It has a front prayer hall for the worship of the Buddha and a rear prayer hall for other deities. The Ling Guangsi was built in the eleventh century AD and rebuilt in AD 1428 and 1478. An octagonal brick pagoda, the Qian Fota 千佛塔, dated AD 1971 is in the east of its courtyard.[19] In this courtyard are many outstanding landscape elements such as a goldfish pond that is over one hundred years old, gilded vessels, and other antiques.

The San Shanan is a small temple while the Da Beisi, dated Ming dynasty, is large and consists of three halls, one of which houses the statues of the Eighteen Arhats. The landscape elements in this temple are fascinating. For example, one of the trees is believed to be over eight hundred years old.

The Long Wangtang is situated northwest of the Da Beisi and its landscape is enhanced by a clear stream that flows from one courtyard to another into a pond. Beyond the pond is the main prayer hall. Fairly close to this temple is the Xiang Jiesi which is raised on high ground and approached by a steep flight of stone steps. The main gate, Da Chengmen, leads to the prayer hall and the sutra storage hall. The central hall of the three, flanked by the bell and drum towers, is for the worship of the Buddha whose icon is flanked by the statues of the Eighteen Arhats.

A mile away from the Xiang Jiesi is the Bao Zhudong which is named because of its *baozhu* (pearl-like) cave stones. In front of the temple is a viewing pavilion from which distant vistas are obtained.

On top of the Lushi hill is an old temple named Zheng Guosi, dated during the Sui dynasty. From the temple a winding path leads to the Mi Moyan, an overhanging cliff which resembles the head of a lion.

The Huang Qiongyu is the former throne of the Imperial Vault of the Heavens used for the worship of Huangtian Shangdi (the Heavenly Emperor). The shrine is flanked by spirit tablets of royal ancestors. The lower building has beautiful latticework windows and doors while the roof structure consists of rings of ornately painted beams and *dougong*. The columns are red with gilded floral patterns.

Bi Yunsi 碧云寺

The Bi Yunsi was reconstructed in AD 1289 and was known as Bi Yunan 碧云庵. It was given its present name in AD 1516. The Qing emperor, Qian Long, added a few temples such as the Jing Cisi 静慈寺. The Tian Wangdian houses a Ming-dated bronze icon of the Buddha. The rear halls are dedicated to the former Nationalist leader, Sun Zhongshan 孙中山.

Tan Zhesi 潭柘寺

The Tan Zhesi was built during the Jin dynasty and then rebuilt and renamed many times during its historical past. Its name relates to the presence of a deep pond and *zhe* trees on the nearby hill. This is a large complex spreading out to the east and west. Along the central axial line are located the main gateway, the first, main and rear prayer halls.

Long Xingsi 龙兴寺

This temple was built at the Zengding Xian of Hebei in the year AD 586. It is a Buddhist temple for the worship of Guan Yin, the Goddess of Mercy. The planning is based on the courtyard concept, involving harmony and balance. The roofs of the main buildings are half-hipped/half-gabled.

The temple of Yong Hegong was originally the residence of the crown prince and was converted into a Lama temple. It is still famous throughout China for its relics, icons and the Luo Hanshan which houses five hundred statues of the Eighteen Arhats.

Du Lesi 独乐寺

This temple is at Jixian in Hebei and it was built in AD 986. Dedicated to Guan Yin and other Buddhist deities it is raised on a stone podium. The structure is of timber and its construction is modelled on the Song beam-frame system.

Tai Yuan Jinci 太原晋伺

Built during the eleventh century at Taiyuan, Shanxi, this temple is used for paying respect to the ancestors. Well-known for its collection of antiques and old sculptures it is dedicated to Xingmu, the saintly mother. The structural system of the temple is truly authentic and classical in style.

Yong Legong 永乐宫

Built at Ruicheng in Shanxi in AD 1262, Yong Legong is a Taoist temple and is dedicated to the Eight Immortals, the saintly figures who achieved immortality during the eighth to ninth century AD. This temple is noted for its paintings and wall murals.

Temples in Beijing

Countless temples have been built in north China, many of these in Beijing: the Tian Ningsi 天宁寺, the Qing Zhensi 清真寺, the Huangsi 黄寺, the Wu Tasi 五台寺 and the Da Zhongsi 大钟寺.

The Liao-dated Tian Ningsi is situated at the north of the Guang Anmen. Its name was given during the Ming dynasty. It is an octagonal thirteen-storey pagoda standing on a square podium which was built as early as the Sui dynasty.

The Qing Zhensi, dated Ming dynasty, is one of Beijing's authentic timber temples while the Huangsi, dated AD 1651, is so named because it is covered with yellow glazed tiles. It is made up of two buildings, one in the east and the other in the west. The west building has three halls and two courtyards. Within the first courtyard are the bell and drum towers. Five building blocks surround the second courtyard.

The five pagodas of the Wu Tasi, dated AD 1473, stand on a large 17-metre-high podium. The pagodas are fashioned upon Indian stupas. The central pagoda is thirteen storeys high while the corner pagodas are eleven storeys high. The temple was renovated in AD 1761 and during the Qing dynasty after it was razed to the ground by foreign invaders.[20]

The Da Zhongsi was built in AD 1733. Its square bell tower with a round top is 16.7 metres high – a well-known temple because when its Ming dynasty bell sounds it can be heard miles away.[21]

Other temples include the Jie Tasi which was built in honour of Sire Vinaya during the Liao dynasty. It was rebuilt in the Ming dynasty. It is raised on high ground and from it a commanding view of the surrounding area can be obtained.

The Zhi Fasi is in the eastern section of the city and was built in AD 1443. The main structures are the *shanmen* 山门 (entrance gate), the drum and bell towers, the entrance gate, the prayer halls and the main prayer halls, the Ru Laidian 如来殿 (Buddha Hall) and the Da Beitang 大悲堂 (Hall of the Goddess of Mercy). In the Ru Laige 如来阁 pavilion there are as many as nine thousand statues. Thus it is also known as Wan Foge 万佛阁 (Pavilion of Ten Thousand Buddhas). The most impressive architectural feature is the coffered ceiling of this pavilion; the most unusual is the use of black glazed tiles for the main buildings.

Built in AD 1651 the Yong Ansi was originally named Bai Tasi 白塔寺. It has a few halls, namely the Fa Lundian 法轮殿, the Zhenju Juedian 正觉殿 and Pu Andian 普安殿. The Wan Shansi is a Buddhist temple for the worship of the Eighteen Arhats, the Goddess of Mercy and the Buddha. The rear hall is named Qian Fodian 千佛殿. There is a octagonal seven-storey pagoda dating back to the Ming dynasty which houses a golden Buddha.

General Observations

Beijing is a large city with thousands of classical buildings and temples. These have been built not only in accordance with traditional practices and styles of architecture but also as houses of the deities with divine powers. Therefore, the architecture is of divine scale and the geometry of these buildings reflects the spiritual powers of the deities. For example, instead of adopting square plans, octagonal or circular shapes are used for the construction of these buildings.

Even though Beijing has undergone thousands of years of development and evolution, the architectural style has not changed to a great extent because it has been constrained by traditional practices, and in the past, by practices based on the feudal system. The stereotyped courtyard concept and structural system has prevailed and has exerted its influence on Chinese temples in the southeast Asian countries, where offshoots of these Chinese temples have been built and the abbots of the temples in the southeastern Asian countries have established close ties with those in China. Religious structures are often modelled upon those constructed in China, if not completely, at least in terms of the use and application of building materials and the concept of space and planning.

The basic planning concept places the entrance called the *shanmen* on the lower level. This *shanmen* leads to the first hall called the Tian Wangdian 天王殿. The second or the third hall is usually the main prayer hall named the Da Xiong Baodian 大雄宝殿. The halls beyond are called the Houdian 后殿 and they are often used by monks as residential quarters and also for ancestor worship. Many temples are built with pagodas as landmarks, or viewing towers and also for the placement of religious relics. The colour schemes and decorative motifs as well as the application of symbolism of the temples are generally based on traditional practices.

Notes

1 See Li Jie 李诫, *Yingzao Fashi* 营造法式, and Wang Yunwu 王云五, op cit, p39.

2 The *si* was originally the place for receiving visiting monks. During the reign of the Han emperor, Ming Di (AD 58-75), two Indian monks brought the Buddhist Classics to China, and they were received at the Hong Lusi 鸿胪寺 (later renamed Bai Masi 白马寺) near Luoyang in Henan.

3 There are exceptions; the Yong Hegong is especially large.

4 Some temples are named after the special relics or icons of Buddha that they house. For example, the Wo Fosi in Beijing houses a huge sleeping Buddha.

5 See Gin Djih Su, *Chinese Architecture – Past and Contemporary* (Hong Kong) 1964, p49.

6 See Wang Yunwu, op cit, pp43-46.

7 Refer to the beam-framed system on p30.

8 Wang Yunwu had collected over three hundred window and opening designs.

9 See Lip, Evelyn, *Chinese Temples and Deities*, Times Books International (Singapore) 1953, pp99-100.

10 See Lip, Evelyn, *Chinese Geomancy*, op cit, pp56-60.

11 Many temples have been constructed in this manner such as the Fo Xiangge.

12 When the temple was first built by the Ming emperor its roofs were azure-green, yellow and green. The colour scheme changed to blue during the Qing dynasty to associate the temple with the heavens.

13 In ancient time the day was divided into twelve double hours: *zi* 子, *chou* 丑, *yin* 寅, *mao* 卯, *chen* 辰, *si* 巳, *wu* 午, *wei* 未, *shen* 申, *you* 酉, *shu* 戌 and *hai* 亥. See Lip, Evelyn, *Chinese Geomancy*, op cit, 1979, p20.

14 The total number of columns is twenty-eight, representing the twenty-eight constellations.

15 There are three stone slabs named San Yinshi 三音石. When a person stands on the first stone slab facing the Zhaigong and claps his hands he hears the echo once. When he stands on the second and third stone slab he can hear the echo twice and thrice respectively.

16 The Huanqiu was built in AD 1530. The northern boundary of the Tiantan is curved while the southern has 90-degree angles because the curve represents the heavens and the right angles the earth.

17 The number 9 was associated with the emperor and was considered as the supreme *yang* number. It was used again and again in the design of the Huanqiu.

18 The built-up area is *yang* and the void is *yin*. There should always be balance between *yin* and *yang* spaces in order to achieve harmony and well-being.

19 See He Kundeng 和坤等, *Rixia Jiuwen Kao* 日下旧闻考, Qing dynasty.

20 See Zhou Shachen 周沙尘, *Gujin Beijing* 古今北京, Joint Publishing Company (Hong Kong) 1980, p159.

21 The bell is over 7 metres high and over 3 metres in diameter.

Landscape Gardens in Beijing and Chengde

Landscape garden design has gone through a long historic phase of development. One of the Confucian classics, the Shijing 诗经 records the construction of imperial gardens during the Zhou dynasty (1066–255 BC). The Qin ruler (third century BC) built huge gardens at the south of the Wei river and the East and West Han rulers did equally well in developing magnificent imperial gardens. During the Three Kingdoms era owing to constant warfare developing, the warlords were concerned with more pressing matters than the landscaping of gardens. However, many cultivated the habit of turning to nature for the rejuvenation of body and spirit. Thus, the love of nature led to the building of more landscape gardens. Moreover, the flourishing of the Buddhist religion in China brought about the construction of countless monasteries and religious centres in settings complete with landscaped gardens.

One of the largest imperial gardens built by the Sui kingdom's Yang Di (AD 605–617) was the Xiyuan 西苑 at Luoyang 洛阳. It was of interest mainly because it was built on undulating ground and the Luo river was fully utilised to supply the huge garden with large lakes and other water features.

The Tang rulers constructed huge imperial palaces complete with magnificent imperial gardens that had all the elements of landscape gardens such as pavilions, corridors, buildings, pagodas, rockeries and lakes. Along with the imperial gardens the building of private gardens flourished. The development of landscape gardens continued and by the Song dynasty (AD 960–1279) the number of gardens in the capital cities multiplied.[1] Hangzhou 杭州, Suzhou 苏州 and Yangzhou 扬州 were centres where garden design reached its climax in theme and variety.

The Yuan rulers were not keen on landscaping gardens but in the Ming dynasty the capital moved to Beijing which had the natural amenity and water supply of the Beihai 北海, the Zhonghai 中海 and the Nanhai 南海. More landscape gardens were developed and many imperial gardens were built.

The techniques and art of landscaping were written in an important work, the *Yuan Yi* by Ji Cheng. The fervour in developing imperial gardens was demonstrated by the Qing emperors, Kang Xi 康熙 and Qian Long 乾隆. The scale, size and richness of detail was at the height of excellence, as seen in the imperial gardens in Beijing and elsewhere such as Yangzhou, Suzhou and Hangzhou.

Classical Landscape Architecture

A successful Chinese classical landscape artist is one who succeeds in making the elements in a garden look as if they are part of nature and in harmony with nature. A successful design must have a sense of poetry and purpose. It must have a composition that consists of:

- *shumi deyi* 疏密得宜 (contrast of openness and closeness);
- *quzhe jinzhi* 曲折尽致 (full of curved and straight lines) and
- *yanqian youjing* 眼前有景 (view and vista in front).

West of the Tian Wangdian is the Ming dynasty Wu Longting, also known as the Five Dragon Pavilion. Each pavilion has a name depicting association with the *yang* dragon and traditional Chinese architecture based on balance and harmony. The main central pavilion, Longze, has an extraordinary circular pyramidal roof over a square pavilion.

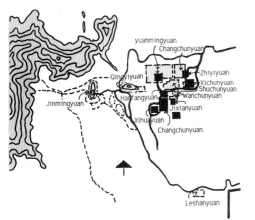

Map of Beijing showing the landscape gardens

Part of the imperial garden from the Liao to Qing eras, the Beihai has been expanded by successive emperors and covers an area of 700,000 square metres, half of which is water.

To achieve these objectives the following techniques have to be applied:

- *zhushan* 筑山 (making hills);
- *lishui* 理水 (creating water) and
- *zhiwu peizhi* 植物配置 (placing elements in appropriate positions).

Therefore, a landscape artist must attempt to contrast the rockeries with the lake (natural or man-made), blend the structures with nature and integrate the man-made forms with the spaces created to render meaning and purpose to the landscape.

Ideally, water from a river, a stream or waterfall is the most desirable element but if a landscape has no natural amenities a man-made lake may be introduced. In such a case the man-made element must be so well-made that it appears absolutely natural.[2] Water without rockeries or hills nearby to give contrast produces little positive effects. Other landscape elements such as pavilions, trees, plants and bridges are also important and they should blend with each other to form a symphony of natural beauty. They should be positioned in such a manner that there are *yin* (negative) and *yang* (positive) forms, solid and void spaces, and there should be harmony, continuity, contrast, balance and rhythm.[3]

Most of all there must be a sense of anticipation and surprise according to the Chinese saying, '*fenghui luzhuan yiwu lu* 峰回路转 疑无路, *liuan huaming you yi chun* 柳暗花明又一春', (When the peak of the hill is reached and the road turns around one thinks that the route has come to an end. But after one has seen the shadow of the willows and the brightness of the flowers one sees yet another village). Gardens are to be designed in such a way that they can be enjoyed.[4] Even the name given to them should be poetic and meaningful.

Although sizeable gardens were built as early as the Qin era, in the third century BC they were rather disorganised in theme. Most of the prominent gardens were built by the government. By the Nanbei Chao (fifth century AD) classical landscape architecture was based on clear principles related to harmony with nature. Many private gardens were built and imperial gardens flourished. The art of landscape was fully developed in the seventh century AD during the Tang dynasty. Large-scale imperial gardens such as the Xiyuan 西苑, and Hua Qinggong 华清宫 were completed, and the development of private gardens flourished. Classical landscape garden development reached its peak during the Song dynasty (AD 960–1279) and continued to develop until the Ming and Qing eras when it reached its golden age. Technical as well as aesthetic skills developed fully. The private gardens outside Beijing flourished in the valley of the Yangzi river and in the cities of Suzhou 苏洲, Hangzhou 杭洲 and Yangzhou 杨洲, while in the northern regions of China and in Beijing, imperial gardens were developed with royal patronage. Emperor Qian Long had five major gardens developed: the Chang Chunyuan 畅春园, the Yuan Mingyuan 圆明园, the Qing Yiyuan 清漪园, the Jing Mingyuan 静明园 and the Jing Yiyuan 静宜园.

Ming and Qing Landscape Gardens

Major imperial gardens in Beijing were constructed during the Ming and Qing dynasties. During the Ming period as many as eighty gardens were created in Beijing.[5] Six imperial gardens were built for the enjoyment of the royal household: the Yu Huayuan 御花园, the Ci Ningyuan 慈宁园, the Jingshan Huanyuan 景山花园, the Xiyuan 西苑, the Dongyuan 东苑 and the Tuyuan 兔园. The Yu Huayuan and the Jingshan Huayuan were built in the north along the main axial line of Beijing, the Ci Ningyuan, the Tuyuan and the Xiyuan in the west and the Dongyuan in the southeast. Of the six gardens Xiyuan was the largest and it was extended during the reign of emperor Tian Shun (AD 1457–1464).[6] Half of the Xiyuan was water-filled and the entry to the garden was through three gateways, namely the Xi Yuanmen 西苑门 (the main gate which was directly opposite the Xi Huamen 西华门 of the Gugong 故宫), the Qian Mingmen 乾明门 and the Zhi Shanmen 陟山门.

The Yu Huayuan was built in AD 1403, sited within the Gugong and situated north of the imperial palace, the Kun Ninggong 坤宁宫. Connected to the imperial palaces, the garden contained many interesting buildings for relaxation and for worship. For example, the Qin Andian was for the worship of Taoist deities. Enclosed by walls it provided privacy and magnificent views of landscape elements and natural plants in a wide variety of colours and shapes.

The Dongyuan and the Xiyuan were sited opposite one another. They were designed to give a sense of the preservation of nature and its beauty. The special water features, waterfalls and lakes with dragon waterspouts, were the main attractions in the Dongyuan. Other interesting features were arched bridges, pavilions and man-made rockeries.

The Tuyuan was designed to give a sense of shelter. Cave-like man-made rockeries were piled up artistically to give a sense of adventure to the visitors. Mid-way up the 'hill' of rockeries there was a cave-like space and a platform for viewing. At the top of the 'hill' a magnificent view could be obtained. To contrast with the 'hill' a lake was built to enhance the *feng shui*.

Although Beijing was partly destroyed when the Qing overthrew the Ming ruler and many parts of Beijing were rebuilt and altered, the Yu Huayuan, the Jing Shanyuan and the Tuyuan remained as they were.

During the reign of emperor Kang Xi 康熙 (AD 1662–1723) several important gardens were developed in the northern suburb of Beijing: the Xiangshan Xinggong 香山行宫, the Cheng Xinyuan 澄心园, the Chang Chunyuan 畅春园, the Xi Huayuan 西花园, the Han Huayuan 含花园, the Jixian Yuan 集贤院, the Xi Chunyuan 熙春园, the Zi Yiyuan 自怡园 and the Yuan Mingyuan 圆明园. Of the gardens mentioned the Yuan Mingyuan was the most important as it was used as a holiday resort residence by emperor Yong Zheng 雍正 who reigned from AD 1723 to 1736. The Chang Chunyuan was second in importance as it was used by the empress as a garden resort. In AD 1725 the Yuan Mingyuan was extended by Yong Zheng and it was given the name of Ligong Yuyuan 离宫御苑. It then covered an area of about 200 hectares and had twenty-eight prominent structures on the site. Based on the theme of '*sanfen shui, erfen zhu, yifen wu*' 三分水, 二分竹, 一分屋 (the ratio of water element to plants and trees and to buildings is three to two to one). The garden is so large in area that during the Qing era it had to be guarded by more than three thousand soldiers when the emperor was in residence.

The development of Chinese gardens continued right through the long reign (AD 1736–1796) of emperor Qian Long 乾隆. Qian Long built many resorts and gardens such as the Qing Qiyuan 清漪园, the Chang Chunyuan 畅春园 and the Yi Chunyuan 漪春园 (now known as Wan Chunyuan 万春园). He made improvements and extensions to many existing gardens such as the Yuan Mingyuan, the Nanyuan and the Xiyuan. In AD 1737 after the major extension of the Yuan Mingyuan had been completed, Qian Long used it as his *ligong* 离宫 (resort palace). The garden complex then had another twelve major structures added to make it a garden with forty resort areas. Each resort area was given a particular name which depicted the mood, the ambience and the poetry of the place. Noted artists such as Shen Yuan 沈源 and Tang Dai 唐岱 were assigned to paint at each scenic spot so that a total of forty paintings were done to portray the spirit of the forty-resort area. Qian Long himself contributed by making poems and recitations on the beauty of the *si shijing* (forty

Lang and *qiang* (corridor and wall)

Pailou (gateway)

Ting (pavilion)

The Le Shoutang is traditionally styled with unique construction details. Steep eaves and verge overhangs are partly supported by rounded beams protruding beyond the tie beams. The columns are red and the walls are intricate latticework panels.

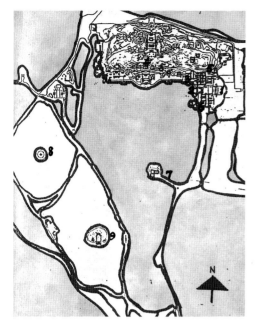

Site plan of the Yi Heyuan

scenic places). The Yuan Mingyuan's main theme of design was based on *shan shui* 山水 (hill and water). A variety of water features was used and the size and depths of each area of water were contrasted, thus large lakes were contrasted with small pools. Yet the lakes seemed to merge with one another. The rich variety of themes, the contrast of *yin* (fluid) and *yang* (solid) elements, the magnificence of scale, the refinement of details and the skilful craftsmanship of the sculptor contributed to the success of Yuan Mingyuan.

The Chang Chunyuan and the Yi Chunyuan were designed with similar themes to the Yuan Mingyuan. There was a total of one hundred and twenty structures in the combined garden complex and yet the building form was not repeated to demonstrate the richness of ideas.

Garden Elements

The essential features in a Chinese garden are *shan* 山 (hill) and *shui* 水 (water). Without such features the garden is incomplete and lacks the contrast of *yin* and *yang* or fluidity and solidity. It is of vital importance that all of the elements are in harmony with one another. As much as possible the man-made elements such as *ting* 亭, *lang* 廊, *qiao* 乔, *fang* 舫, *ta* 塔 and *pailou* 牌楼 and natural elements such as hills, rockeries, stones, streams (or rivers, lakes and pools), flowers and trees must be present to make the garden complete.

Ting, or pavilions, give shelter against the forces of nature and provide a sheltered spot for visitors to rest and view their surroundings.[7] The *ting* can be round, square or other geometric shapes. They may be surrounded by water and linked by bridges, partially surrounded by water, or may be on flat land or on hilly ground.

The *lang* is a covered corridor giving shelter against adverse weather conditions while also allowing a definite direction of circulation and direction of view. There are various types of *lang*: some are roofed, some enclosed or left open.[8]

The *qiao*, or bridge, provides a link from the land area over the lake or pool to the pavilion or to another part of the garden. It may be long and require feats of engineering or may be small and built of timber. Some bridges are ornamental, some arched, some flat and some incorporate pavilions.[9]

The *fang* is also called *chuanting* because it is built to look like a boat. In effect, it is like a pavilion on water as it serves as a resting and viewing platform.[10] The *ta* is a pagoda and usually has many levels. It is regarded as a landmark and sometimes houses relics.[11]

The *qiang* is a garden wall used for screening and for directing or focusing on specific vistas in the garden. It may be solid, consist of a latticework frame or may contain many openings of various shapes and sizes.

The *pailou* marks the entrance of a garden.[12] Most imperial gardens have elaborate garden gateways that carry signboards or poetic inscriptions. Signboards are important elements because the appropriate design or inscription has auspicious implications.

Hills, rockeries and stones are solid elements. They are used as backdrops and to provide contrast with other elements. Streams, rivers and lakes are liquid, fluid and intuitive elements and they give *qi* (energy) and life to the garden landscape. Flowers, plants and trees are decorative and bring life and colour to the garden. Most flowering and non-flowering plants are seasonal and are specially grown and located according to their ecology. Their texture, colour, shape and size are all designed to enhance not just the harmony but also the contrast of the whole environment in the garden.[13]

Yi Heyuan 颐和园, the Summer Palace

The Yi Heyuan stands on the site of the former Qing Yiyuan 清漪园 which was destroyed in AD 1860. In AD 1750 emperor Qian Long had the Qing Yiyuan built to the northwest of Beijing. The site was specially designed for the garden complex with the Wan Shoushan as the hilly backdrop and the Kun Minghu 昆明湖 in front as the desirable water element.[14] The *feng shui* of the place was considered ideal. It took fifteen years to complete the former Qing Yiyuan. Unfortunately, in AD 1860 during the reign of emperor Xian Feng, the Qing Yiyuan was burnt to the ground by the British. It was left in a state of ruin until AD 1898 when Cixi, the empress dowager of the last Qing emperor, used the navy's expenditure and maintenance fund to reconstruct it. Thus, Yi Heyuan was completed in time to celebrate the sixtieth birthday of the empress dowager. When it was razed to the ground in AD 1860 only a few structures, the Bronze Pavilion, the Sea of Wisdom Tower and the Glazed Tile Pagoda, remained standing. In AD 1900 the garden was devastated by the troops of foreign powers but Cixi had it restored again in AD 1902.

The design of the Yi Heyuan garden complex was based on 'san shan wu yuan' 三山五院 (three hills for five courtyards), and it was modelled on the design of Hangzhou's Xihu 西湖. Many varieties of trees were planted but pine trees dominated the garden as they symbolise longevity. Lotus grew in the lakes; and, along the lakeside, willows and cherry trees were planted.

Sited on the northwest of Beijing, Yi Heyuan covers an area of about three square kilometres of which three-quarters are covered by the lake. It was used as the residence and administrative office of the empress dowager. The design objectives of the reconstructed garden complex were thus as follows:

• As much as possible the structures that could be retained were renovated. Names of residential palaces were changed according to the functions they served.

• Destroyed multi-storey structures were converted to single storey (possibly to reduce cost).

• Whenever necessary and possible, spaces were extended and new structures were added to accommodate the activities required by the empress dowager.

The main entrance gate to Yi Heyuan is the eastern gate called Dong Gongmen 东宫门 which has a man-made stream flowing across its front court symbolising 'wealth brought into the royal household'. The wooden entrance gateway, the Ren Shoumen 仁寿门, has round wooden posts supporting the intricate *dougong* (brackets) and the roof structure. This gateway leads to the courtyard of the Ren Shoudian 仁寿殿 (Hall of Benevolence and Longevity) in which numerous ornamental objects, incense burners, bronze peacocks, dragons, lions, deer and unicorns are displayed. The incense burners were once used to make joss offerings to the heavens. The bronze peacocks and dragons signify the *yin* and *yang* qualities that render balance and harmony. The lions are *yang* and represent strength; deer symbolise wealth; and the unicorn is a symbol of wisdom.

The interior of the Ren Shoudian is ornately decorated. Its coffered ceiling is beautifully painted in green, blue and red while its columns are red. Its doors are exquisitely made with lattice infills framed by solid timber. In the centre of the hall is a dais on which is placed an intricately carved imperial seat of *hua limu* 花梨木 with yellow cushions. Behind the seat is an elaborately carved screen and a pair of fans made from peacock feathers and with gilded handles. Around the throne are placed many antique pieces such as crane-shaped lanterns, enamelled tripods and gilded incense burners.

The Zhi Huihai, a brick and stone-built Lama temple, has unique elevations consisting of arches and walls of vividly colourful glazed tiles. The roof ridges are finished with glazed green and yellow ceramic sculptures. The external walls have rows of recessed niches housing over one thousand small statues of Buddha.

The charm of the Kun Minghu lies in the vast expanse of calm water, reflecting the natural and architectural form of Longevity Hill. Originally called Golden Water Pond the lake was increased in the twelfth century when emperor Zhang Zong channelled water from the Yuhushan.

One of the main architectural features in the Yi Heyuan, the Seventeen-Arched Bridge is built of stone and spans 150 metres over the Kun Minghu.

The importance of the Pai Yundian, built to celebrate Cixi's sixtieth birthday, is expressed in the powerful symbolic detailing: the yellow two-tier, half-hipped/half-gabled roof; seven mythical animals on the roof corners; its marble podium and balusters with carved lotus details; and the seven-bay front elevation.

A number of palaces were built for the relaxation of the empress dowager, Cixi, including the Le Shoutang 乐寿堂 (Hall of Happiness in Longevity). A large complex planned with several courtyards, it was used by Cixi for residence and as such was lavishly furnished. The throne room had a subdued colour scheme, its rosewood furniture contrasting starkly with the gilded incense burners, and other ornaments. The bedroom was tastefully furnished with stained rosewood antique furniture, jadeite and precious stones, exquisite embroidery and art works. The elevation of the building appears simple and well-proportioned and also utilises a subdued colour scheme.

West of the Le Shoutang and between the Ren Shoudian and the stone boat is the Changlang, the Long Gallery, which was constructed in AD 1860. It is 728 metres long with rafters carved and painted with different themes, symbols and landscapes. Along this long gallery are four large double-eaved octagonal pavilions.

The Wan Shoushan 万寿山 (Longevity Hill), the focal point of the Summer Palace, is on the north side of the gallery, where the most interesting buildings are grouped. Most prominent is the four-storey eight-sided Fo Xiangge 佛香阁 (Pavilion of the Buddha's Fragrance) which faces the Kun Minghu. It is covered with yellow glazed tiles and supported by red columns. Sited on the highest part of the hill, it can be reached by steep stone staircases. The 40-metre tower is skilfully built in timber and superbly detailed.

Behind the Fo Xiangge are the Lama Temples, the Bai Yundian 白云殿 (Hall of Clouds) and the Zhi Huihai 智慧海 (Sea of Wisdom). The Zhi Huihai is a two-storey masonry building constructed without beams and rafters, and is covered with yellow and green glazed tiles.[15]

At the verge of the Kun Minghu is a wooden gateway which frames the gateway of the temple complex. To the west of Longevity Hill is the 6-metre bronze pavilion, Bao Yunge 宝云阁, which was built in AD 1750 with bronze castings made by Jesuit priests.[16] Even though the pavilion was cast in bronze its appearance is that of timber. Its roof is half-hipped/half-gabled and its roof ridge centre carries a *baoding* (precious capping) with an umbrella-like ornament. Its windows are open, without latticework.

Climbing down the hill the pavilion for listening to the Orioles can be reached. It was used as a theatre during the Qing dynasty.[17] To the east of Fo Xiangge are libraries for the storage of sutras.

Turning south from the entrance, the South Lake Islands can be reached. A tower named Wen Zhangge 文章阁 (Pavilion of Literature) which honours the God of Literature is sited on the shore path to the Iron Ox built by emperor Qian Long in AD 1755. The seventeen-arched Kongqiao 孔桥 (Confucius bridge) links the east end of the path to the South Island and the Taoist Long Huangmiao 龙皇庙 (Dragon King Temple) which is dedicated to the dragon kings who were believed to rule the four seas. The Kongqiao is beautifully arched with marble balustrades topped with about five hundred stone lion heads. The bridge is finished with marble slabs.

Walking towards the north, the Yi Ledian 颐乐殿 (Hall of Happiness) and the Yu Langtang 玉浪堂 (Hall of Jade Wave) can be reached. The Yi Ledian was built as a Chinese opera stage for the amusement of the empress dowager, Cixi. The Yu Langtang was for viewing the beautiful lake.

The Kanyu of the Yi Heyuan

When the Yi Heyuan was planned it was the perfect *kanyu* setting for a retirement and pleasure park for Cixi. It had the solidity of the Wan Shoushan (Longevity Hill) behind and the necessary *shui* (water of the Kun Minghu) to provide the perfect balance of *yin* (water) to *yang* (hill) and also superb vistas and views. As early as the

Built in AD 1891, De Heyuan was the best equipped opera stage of the era, with its lowest stage 17 metres wide and featuring five fountains below stage for scenes requiring water features.

The beams of the Changlang are painted with over fourteen thousand vivid illustrations that relate historical and religious legends and record China's natural beauty.

The residence of the penultimate Qing emperor, Guang Xu, Yu Langtang has a splendid interior with exquisite and skilfully carved throne furniture in front of a beautiful painted screen.

Sketch of Wan Shoushan.

In the foreground of this sketch of Yi Heyuan, is the South Lake Island facing the Wan Shoushan. This island was purposely created to complement the *feng shui* of the Wan Shoushan or Longevity Hill. Directly facing Longevity Hill is the Han Xutang which is built in the traditional style raised on solid rocks.

Yuan dynasty the Kun Minghu was dredged and the spring water from the Weng Shan was diverted into the Tonghui He. The site therefore had the balance of the *yin* and *yang* elements as spelt out by the signs opposite its entrance gateway which read '*Hanxu*' 涵虚 and '*Yanxiu*' 罨秀. *Hanxu* implied there was water in the park and *Yanxiu* referred to the hills.

The main buildings in the Yi Heyuan are: the Fo Xiangge, the Pai Yundian, the Le Shoutang, the De Heyuan 德合园 and the Xuni Lingjing 须祢灵境. All of the buildings are symmetrically planned based on the courtyard concept. They are enclosed by walls to ensure the *feng shui* of the environment is always constant and unaffected by the elements outside their compound. The Fo Xiangge has the 'backing' of the Wan Shoushan and being on a higher level provides a backdrop to the Pai Yundian.

The Fo Xiangge and the Pai Yundian were once used to hold important religious rituals and ceremonies. They were positioned on the most auspicious and commanding site on the hillside overlooking the lake. The main complex was flanked on the left and right by high ground and buildings which symbolised the 'Azure Dragon' and the 'White Tiger'. The South Lake Island was positioned in such a way that it represented the 'Red Bird'. The seventeen-arched bridge links the *qi* 气 (earth's energy) from the east bank to the South Lake Island in a harmonious and graceful manner. The Xuni Lingjing was built on the hillside in a perfectly balanced and symmetrical formation ventilated through courtyards. In the northern part of the island an artificial hill was built so that the Han Xutang 含畜堂 could be sited on an auspicious site.

Many structures, symbols and sculptures were constructed in the Yi Heyuan to enhance the *feng shui* and the metaphysical environment. The marble boat named Qin Ganfang 清安舫 (the Boat of Purity and Ease) built in AD 1855 on the west bank of the Kun Minghu symbolised 'peaceful sailing' which implied that the ruler of the dynasty would enjoy continued support and success.

Bronze lions, unicorns and dragons were placed to guard the *feng shui* of the imperial garden. Gilded cranes, elephants and bronze deer symbolised longevity, wisdom and fortune respectively. Countless numbers of paintings depicting auspicious themes are painted on the beams of the Changlang to depict prosperity, longevity and happiness. The Changlang itself is a symbol of longevity.

Natural elements such as plants and trees were carefully nurtured and placed to give meaningful significance to the garden. *Yulan* was planted in the courtyard of the Hall of Happiness in Longevity for its beauty and its auspicious symbolism. Pine, cypress and bamboo were planted because they represented longevity and youthfulness. Endurance and purity were signified by the lotus and water lilies grown in the ponds and lakes.

The colour scheme of the buildings and building elements was auspicious as the *yin* colours (blue and green) were used to contrast vividly with the *yang* colours (yellow, red and gold). The structural beams were painted with symbols including dragons, phoenix and symbols representing longevity, fortune and happiness. Ceilings too were painted with auspicious symbols. The window latticework was intricately designed with images of potent symbols such as *ren* 人 (man), *kou* 口 (mouth) for posterity and *tian* 田 (paddy fields) for wealth.

Symbols were not just applied on decorative elements but also on structural elements such as the beams, columns and roofs. The beams and columns were painted in auspicious red and gold colours and multi-coloured patterns or geometrical forms. The roofs were covered with bamboo tiles signifing longevity. Even the edge tiles were moulded with patterns or words of good tiding. The roof ridges were terminated with symbols such as the *shouwen* to portray success.

Plan of Xie Quyuan

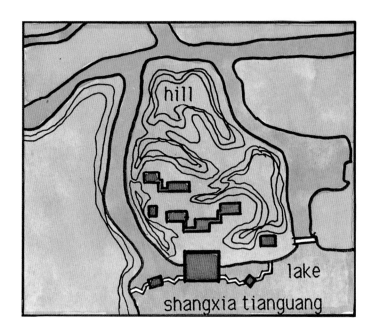

The Shangxia Tianguang nestle amidst the hills but the main building of the group faces the lake with the hills behind. The zig-zag bridge formation eliminates *shaqi* or undesirable, excessively vibrant energy.

Tianran Tuhua

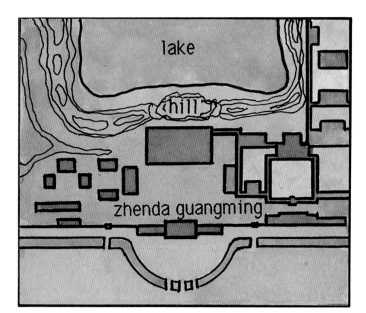

Zhenda Guangming

The Yi Heyuan, indeed, has all the physical features conceived according to the metaphysical system of thought with hills at its rear and lakes in front. The structures on Wan Shoushan are sited according to their importance and hierarchy. The temples, the houses of the deities, are on the highest level. Palaces are on the lower level. The assertion of imperial power is felt in the vastness and grandeur of scale of the estate and palaces. The ornate decoration, furnishing and finishing of the palaces truly reflects the luxurious lifestyle of the empress dowager Cixi, whose gracious living must be demonstrated by such splendid furnishing and precious jewels.

The Xie Quyuan

Situated to the east of the Wan Shoushan, the Xie Quyuan 谐趣园 was built in AD 1751 by emperor Qian Long. It was one of Qian Long's favourite gardens because it was scenic and serene. It had the advantage of having the view of the Wan Shoushan and the peacefulness of the thick wooded garden as well as lakes and refined buildings. It was known as Wei Shanyuan when first completed but it was renamed by emperor Jia Qing 嘉庆 in AD 1811. Burnt to the ground in AD 1860 by the British and rebuilt by emperor Guang Xu 光绪 in AD 1892, it continues to be maintained even today.

From the west and main entrance of Xie Quyuan the view of the beautiful lake can be seen. The first and second pavilions are named Zhi Chunting 知春亭 and Yinjing 引镜 respectively. Beyond the pavilions are two more beautiful pavilions named Xiqiu 洗秋 and Yinlu 饮绿. These were formally named by Qian Long as Shuileting 水乐亭. A bridge provides an alternative route to the Zhi Chuntang 知春堂. The path from the entrance to the exit provides various vistas and creates a sense of anticipation and curiosity. The variety of building forms and shapes enhances the design of the garden. There are square, rectangular, round and octagonal pavilions. Some verandas are built along the lake side, some provide vistas on both sides, some are semi-enclosed and some follow geometric shapes.

The Yuan Mingyuan

The present Yuan Mingyuan situated northwest of Beijing has lost its magnificence and is no longer the greatest of the gardens in China. However, what remains reminds visitors of its glorious past and its beauty when it was first built in AD 1710 by emperor Kang Xi (AD 1662–1723) for his son, Yong Zheng. At that time Yuan Mingyuan was amidst four other great gardens built by Kang Xi. It was designed with over thirty scenic spots complete with ting 亭 (pavilions), lang 廊 (covered corridors), louge 楼阁 (buildings and outhouses) and exquisite plants.

During the reign of Qian Long the Yuan Mingyuan was extended and merged with the Chang Chunyuan and Wan Chunyuan (formerly known as Yi Chunyuan). By the time the extension was completed there were as many as forty scenic areas and groups of buildings; it contained lou 楼 (buildings), tai 台 (raised platforms), dian 殿 (temples), ge 阁 (outhouses and pavilions), zhai' 斋 (meditation areas for vegetarians), fang 肪 (stone boats), tang 堂 (halls), ta 塔 (pagodas) and ting 亭 (pavilions). Each scenic area was like a garden within a garden.

The plants, trees and other natural elements in the Yuan Mingyuan were specially selected and grown. At the peak of its development there were as many as three hundred gardeners to take care of the countless varieties of plants and to provide superb maintenance. The royal patronage of the garden is evident as it has over five thousand signboards with calligraphy executed by the emperors themselves. As many as two hundred poems were written about the beauty of the garden.

Sketches showing some of the roof forms of buildings in the Yuan Mingyuan:

The *shiziding* of the Wanfang Anhe

The *tianziding* of the Yanpo Ningjing

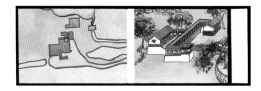

The asymmetrical roof of the Shuimu Mingse

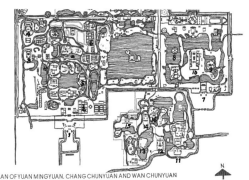

PLAN OF YUAN MINGYUAN, CHANG CHUNYUAN AND WAN CHUNYUAN

Plan of the Yuan Mingyuan

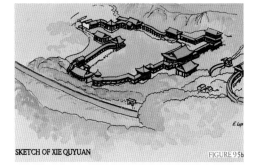

SKETCH OF XIE QUYUAN   FIGURE 95b

Sketch of Xie Quyuan

From research material we have learnt that the pine, the bamboo, the willow and the lotus were used to express the main themes of the garden. Forty per cent of the entire garden compound is covered with water lotus plants which are seen everywhere, colours ranging from golden to white and red. Water, the main element and theme of the garden, creates a rich menu of contrast and sense of anticipation. The visitor is engaged with an endless variety of vistas as he walks from one place to another in the garden.

Indeed, the Yuan Mingyuan did fulfil all the requirements expected of the best imperial gardens. Just as the author of the *Yuan Yi*, Ji Cheng has said, it was masterfully designed with the appropriate trees and plants located in their respective locations to give the best view and to enhance the entire environment. Peony were planted around the buildings, bamboo was grown to surround the outhouses, pine trees in the courtyards and willows on the shores of lakes. Every natural element was used to blend harmoniously with the man-made elements. As a result forty scenic settings like landscape paintings, complete with buildings and gardens, were created.

The Bishu Shanzhuang in Chengde

About 256 kilometres away from Beijing is Chengde, a historical city lying on the Yan Shan 燕山. The most famous cultural and scenic area in Chengde is the Bishu Shanzhuang 避署山庄 (mountain resort in summer). This resort is one of China's ten most scenic spots and it was a very important summer resort for seven out of ten of the Qing rulers. Its construction was initiated by emperor Kang Xi in AD 1703 and expanded by emperor Qian Long until AD 1792.[18] This summer resort covers an area of 5,640,000 square metres and contains three hundred and eighty-four buildings.

Kang Xi ordered a 10-metre-high wall to be built to enclose the entire compound. For the purpose of administration a formal palace complex, covering 24,000 square metres, was built just beyond the Li Zhenmen.

This complex consists of twenty-six existing buildings. Therefore, from Li Zhenmen to Xiu Yunmen the palace buildings, planned in accordance with feudal rites based on the courtyard concept, enclose nine successive internal courtyards. The most important buildings are placed along the central axial line.

The entry to the imperial courtyard is through the Wumen 午门 (Meridian Gate). The inner meridian gateway bears the elaborately-framed signboard '*Bishu Shanzhuang*' which was written by Kang Xi himself. Looking across the open courtyard the Danbo Jingchengdian 澹泊敬诚殿 (Hall of Sincerity) can be seen. This palatial building, being the main hall of administration, is raised from the ground, is built entirely of *nanmu* and has a tastefully furnished throne complete with all the necessary ornaments that reflect imperial authority and power. The hall is designed with nine bays and is covered with a half-hipped/half-gabled roof supported by natural *nanmu*. Panels and beams are intricately carved with auspicious symbols. A courtyard separates the Danbo Jingchengdian from a study, the Sizhi Shuwu (Study of Four Knowledges). Beyond the study is the Yanbo Zhishuangdian 烟波致爽殿 (Hall of Interesting Mist and Wave), the residential palace. This has a seven-bay elevation and it is covered by a curved roof.

At the Western Chamber two Qing emperors passed away – Jia Qing 嘉庆 (in 1820) and Xian Feng 咸丰 (in 1861). Beyond the residential quarters is the Yunshan Shengdi 云山胜地 (Beautiful Hill and Cloud) which is a tower with five bays. Almost parallel to this main palace complex is another group of courtyard buildings beyond which the land slopes down to the lake area.

The lake area covers an area of 30 hectares and is subdivided into eight lakes of various sizes by bridges, dykes and islands. The eastern part has the Yinhu 银湖 (Silver Lake) and the Jinhu 金湖 (Gold Lake) and is highlighted by various features such as the Shui Xinxi 水心榭 (Mid-Lake Pavilions), the Qingshu Shanguan 清舒山馆 (Peaceful Mountain Abode), the Shi Zilin 师子林 (Grove for Lion), the Wenyuan 文园 (Garden of Literature) and Jie Detang 节德堂 (Hall of Charity) and the Hua Shenmiao 花神庙 (Temple of the Flower Fairy).

Three pavilions, named Shui Xinxi, stand on a causeway that separates the Yinhu 银湖 from the Xiahu 下湖 (Lower Lake).

The most interesting and exciting architecturally is the group of structures on the Jinshan 金山 (Gold Hill) on an isle between the Chenghu 澄湖 (Clear Lake) and the Jinhu in the east. On its western fringe is a vestibule linked to the ferry landing by a curved flight of stone steps.

Connected to the vestibule is the Jingshui Yuncen Dian 镜水云岑殿 (Palace of Calm Water and Cloud). The elevation of this palatial hall has five bays and it is covered with a half-hipped/half-gabled roof. Stone steps link the hall to the three-tiered pavilion named Jin Shanta 金山塔 (Pagoda of the Gold Hill). Another pavilion, the Fang Zhouting 芳州亭 (Fragrant Isle Pavilion) is on the north of the island.

A compound named Yan Yuluo 烟雨楼 consisting of structures forming three courtyards is sited on an island and linked to the Ruyi 如意 Island to make up the central part in the lake area. Numerous courtyard buildings are sited on Ruyi Island which is linked by a dyke to an island on which a group of buildings form an interesting courtyard. Along the shore of the Ruyi Hu 如意湖 (Lake of Wishes Come True) and the Chenghu are the Fang Yuanju and several interesting structures and pavilions.

A pleasant walk from the shore of the Ruyi Hu leads to the Meng Gubao 蒙古包 (fashioned upon the Mongolian tents) and the Yong Youta 永佑塔 (Pagoda of Eternal Blessing), a stone pagoda. Further north from here are sited numerous groups of buildings based on the courtyard concept. West of the Meng Gubao is an elongated island on which the notable building, the Wen Jinge 文津阁 (Pavilion of Literature) is situated. Here the Qing emperor used to store his collection of important paintings and classics. This former imperial library was one of the most important during the Qing dynasty.

The western side of the Bishu Shanzhuang is hilly with sheer cliffs and secluded valleys. Several temples such as the Bifeng Si 碧峰寺 occupy hilly sites and wooded areas protected by luxuriant trees.

The Feng Shui of the Bishu Shanzhuang

The *feng shui* of this summer retreat seems almost perfect because of its scenic beauty and serene environment. There is contrast of *yin* (lake, stream, valley and shaded areas) and *yang* (land, causeway, hill and sunlit areas). Bridges span the lakes linking *qi* 气 (energy) from one to the other. Waterside pavilions provide shelter and are a source of *qi* from the lake. Winding corridors linking adjoining buildings channel ever-changing vistas. The rich pastoral aspect of wooded grassland, crags, hills and valleys provides a refreshing environment for rejuvenation.

The islands, lakes and buildings are given auspicious names. For example, the Jinshan (Gold Hill), the Ruyi Hu (Lake of Wishes Come True), the Wen Jinge (Pavilion of Literature). In fact the buildings and scenic spots were personally named by the emperors Kang Xi and Qian Long. The imperial palace complexes could, however, have been better sited so that their back would not be towards the lakes. It would be more desirable that the front faced the lakes with the hills to the rear.

Built in AD 1703 the Jinshan (Gold Hill) is modelled upon the Jin Shansi in Zhenjiang, Jiangsu Province. The hill and walkways are lined with rocks and the view from the top level of the three-tier pavilion is most picturesque.

The Shui Xinxi, built in AD 1709, is also known as the Mid-Lake Pavilions. The central pavilion is covered with a two-tiered roof, the highest a half-hipped / half-gabled roof. Other pavilions are covered with square pyramidal roofs.

The beautiful timber pagoda and rockery on Jinshan

At 65-metres high, Yong Youta is a landmark in the Bishu Shanzhuang. Built in AD 1754, of stone, it is modelled upon the Pagoda of Six Harmonies in the garden of Hangzhou.

Summary

Based on the Taoist ideas of intuition and freedom, Chinese landscape design is unique and quite different from Western design. Unlike the formal and systematic Western approach, Chinese garden design focuses on harmony and contrast between *yin* and *yang*. A landscape garden should be as intuitive as a brush painting. There must be *shan* (solid) and *shui* (liquid), decorated spaces and voids, buildings and courtyards, land and water, covered corridors and exposed paths, arched bridges and zig-zag links as well as tall structures such as pagodas and single storey pavilions.

A sense of anticipation and excitement must be present in a well-conceived garden design. The options for designers are:

- to contrast large open spaces with small semi-covered spaces to dramatise the sense of space;
- to connect zig-zag narrow corridors to open spaces with unlimited views;
- to locate pavilions behind rockeries or thick wooded areas to create a sense of surprise;
- to use walls and other elements to enclose or to act as backdrops of other elements;
- to create contrast by grouping or dispersing elements of design;
- to create rhythm in the design of spaces, the location of garden elements and the planting of trees and flowers;
- to create a sense of light and shade in terms of building details and colour scheme;
- to create differences between levels of topography and floors of buildings;
- to create perspectives and borrowed vistas.

The best garden design is one with natural amenities such as lakes, rivers, hills and undulating ground.

In addition to creating contrast, a sense of balance and harmony is also important. Invariably, a focal point must be created. For example, in the Yi Heyuan, the Fo Xiangge on the Wan Shoushan is a focal point and provides an effective backdrop to the entire garden. Yi Heyuan is also a good example of a well-conceived garden complex that offers a countless variety of spatial experiences ranging from the sense of anticipation and surprise, of multi-directional perspectives to magnificence in scale and vistas. From the corridor of the Fo Xiangge, there is a magnificent panorama of the garden, the Kun Minghu, the Kongqiao and the surrounding scenery.

Landscape gardens in Beijing that fulfil the above criteria are: the Yi Heyuan, the Yuan Mingyuan, the Xie Quyuan, the Chang Chunyuan, the Wan Chunyuan, the Jing Yiyuan, the Qing Yiyuan, the Jing Mingyuan and some private gardens. These gardens are unlike traditional Western landscape design in which spaces and elements are based on geometry and symmetry; Eastern traditional landscape spaces and elements are modelled on nature.

Landscape gardens are, however, incomplete without architectural spaces. In contrast to landscape spaces, these are modelled on Confucian principles based on Taoist ideas. Landscape and architectural elements are combined with natural spaces in harmonious settings to accentuate the beauty and intuitive quality of nature, similar to the qualities of a Chinese brush painting.

Basically there are two approaches to the design concept of spaces – inward-looking and outward-looking. The inward-looking spatial concept is expressed in the courtyard of the traditional *si heyuan* house. Buildings are used to encircle the interior court which is landscaped to provide relief, ventilation and amenity to the enclosed spaces of the buildings. The courtyard is landscaped with elements such as fountains, pools, rockeries, flowers and trees placed in a setting of harmonious composition. If possible a water course is brought from a natural or artificial source to pass the front gate or door to symbolise wealth and luck.

The outward-looking spatial concept of landscape gardens gives the viewer the added advantage of benefiting from the natural beauty of the immediate or the distant landscape that surrounds the buildings.

To enhance this spatial concept the designer makes use of the high and low land forms, the man-made and natural water courses, rockeries and plants to create vistas of beauty and harmony and senses of surprise and anticipation.

Chinese architectural form and space has always been achieved and influenced by Chinese beliefs, culture, philosophies, and physical and natural environment. It is closely related to the beliefs and philosophies of Confucius and Lao Zi. Both Confucian and Taoist philosophies, however, advocate a sense of balance of the negative (*yin*) and positive (*yang*) qualities as expressed in landscape design. Built-up areas contrast with voids, and small areas are compared with large areas. Landscape elements are moulded to express *chang* (hidden) and *lu* (exposed) as well as *she* (void) and *shi* (solid). The skilful designer is able to express both opposite elements in a sensitive and intuitive way so that within the exposed there is a hidden element.

As stated earlier the contrast of solid and void can be achieved in many ways. For example, rocks and hills are solid landscape elements while water and pools are the opposite. Careful placement of these elements to give balance, harmony and contrast enhances the design. Within the solid rockeries voids are created in set-backs below protruding portions. On the lake there are rocks and bridges appearing above the level of the water. The bridges may be in various contrasting forms (straight or zig-zag). Scenery may be viewed from various points of perspective. Buildings such as pavilions, corridors and pagodas are used to further enhance the sense of solid (*yang*) and void (*yin*) expressions. In the northern part of China, buildings that are used to enclose a landscape space are laid out in a more symmetrical formation whereas in the south they are intuitively placed and usually asymmetrical. Comparatively, the northern Chinese landscape gardens are larger and more colourful than those in the south. Some landscape gardens such as the Yuan Mingyuan and Chang Chunyuan are set in large areas of water. Moreover, in the Chinese landscape, buildings play an important role in defining the space; man-made structures combine with natural elements to form an integral whole.

Notes

1 See Li Gefei, *Luoyang Mingyuan Ji*, Song dynasty.

2 This requirement is stipulated in the ancient text Rixia Jiu Wenkao 日下旧闻考, section 26.

3 See Ji Cheng 计成, *Yuan Yi* 圆冶 (China) Ming dynasty. To achieve contrast and interest, gardens were built on hilly sites, preferably on undulating ground with lakes complementing the garden landscape.

4 Guo Xi 郭熙 , a Song writer, in *Linquan Gaozhi* 林泉高致 commented that a landscape garden should be enjoyed by walking through it.

5 See Liu Tong 刘侗 and Yu Yi Zheng 于奕正, *Dijing Jing Wu Lue* 帝京景物略 (China) Ming dynasty.

6 See Zhou Wei Quan 周维权, *Zhongguo Gudian Yuanlin Shi* 中国古典园林史, Mingwen Shuju 明文书局 (Taiwan) 1991, p139. See also Liu Ruo Yu 刘若愚, *Minggong Shi* 明宫史, Ming dynasty.

7 There are as many as forty *ting* or pavilions in the Yi Heyuan.

8 The Changlang 长廊 along the shore of the Kun Minghu of the Yi Heyuan is 728 metres long, incorporates four octagonal pavilions and has two hundred and seventy-three-bays.

9 There are about thirty bridges in the Yi Heyuan, and each one is different.

10 The marble *fang* of the Yi Heyuan resembles a huge boat.

11 The Fo Xiangge in the compound of the Yi Heyuan was originally to be nine storeys.

12 The design of a *pailou* varies according to their importance and functional requirement. Some are just simple gateways while others have bracketing *dougong* that support elaborate roof structures.

13 Hilltops are to be planted with pines and cypresses while the lakes and ponds with lotus, and the shores with willows.

14 Kun Minghu was known as Xihu and was relatively small. It expanded east and north until it reached the foot of Longevity Hill. Islands and causeways were built on the Kun Minghu, adding interest, creating scenic spots and linking all the design elements to form an integrated harmonious composition. See p99 for the layout of Yuan Mingyuan and also p96 for the sketches of the Yi Heyuan and the Wan Shoushan.

15 Lama Buddhism was the national religion during the Qing dynasty of which the emperor was the patron.

16 The castings were made using wax moulds. The names of the artisans were engraved on steles.

17 Cixi loved the theatre and Beijing opera. Her three hundred and eighty-four-member opera troupe was in constant attendance. See Beijing Summer Palace Administration Office and the Department of Qinghua University, *Summer Palace*, Zhaohua Publishing House (Beijing) 1981, p21.

18 Before the summer resort was built Kang Xi had the habit of retreating to a Lamaist sanctuary to escape the summer heat for three months. See Qing dynasty record *Qiju Zhuche* 起居注册. After the resort was built he stayed there from May to October each year. See Tianjin Daxue Jianzhu Xi 天津大学建筑系, *Chengde Gu Jianzhu* 成德古建筑, *Chengde shiwen Wuju* 成德市文物局, China Building Industry Press (China) 1980, p3.

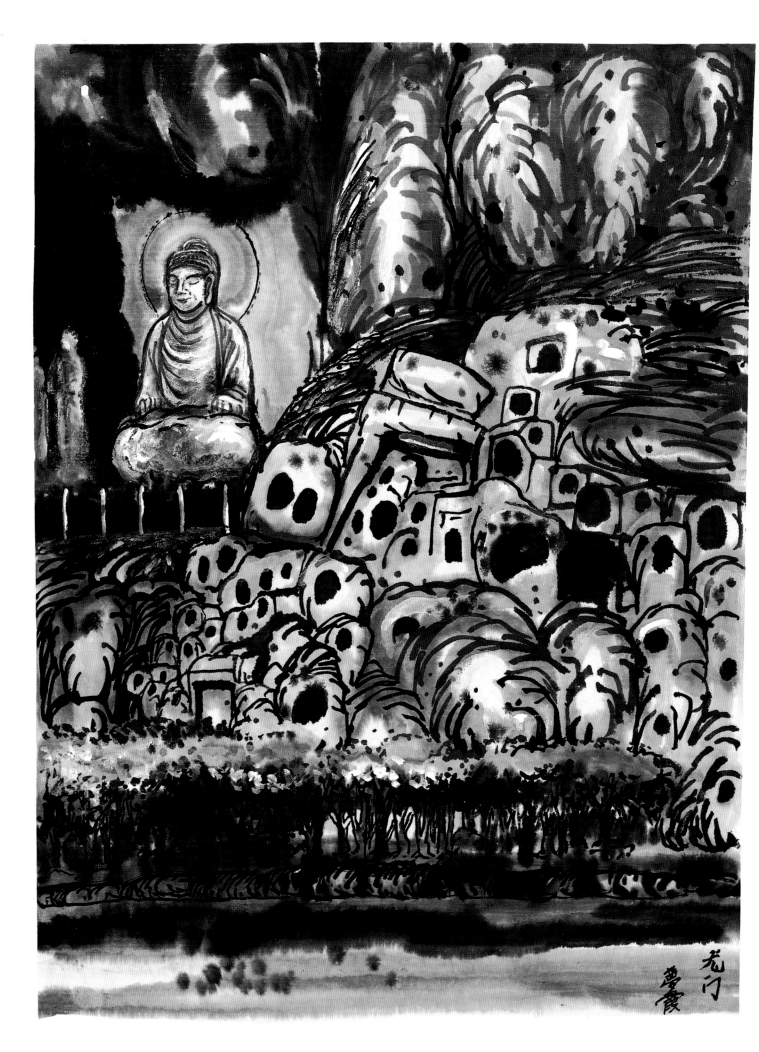

Luoyang

Luoyang is now an agricultural and industrial city in Henan 河北. It sits on the north shore of the Huang He 黄河 and its city centre is crossed by the Luo He 洛河. The Luo Yangqiao 洛阳乔 bridges over the Luo He and leads the way to the Ding Ding Road, to the west of which is the Zhong Zhou Road. North of this road is the Luoyang Museum. On the east is the old city and further east is the famous Bai Masi. Luoyang has the Mang Hill to its north although it is generally flat.

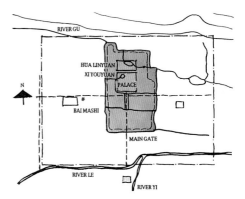

Luoyang dates back to the Neolithic period (5,000 BC), but its name then was Luo 雒. It was the capital of the Shang dynasty (1523–1066 BC) and continued to be the seat of government during the Zhou dynasty (1066–256 BC). During the East Zhou era it was established as the capital.[1] When Qinshi Huangdi (246–209 BC) ruled China it was not the capital but remained an important city.[2] During the Warring States era (481–221 BC) Luo (Luoyang) was the capital of the Zhou domain.[3]

The first emperor of the Later or East Han dynasty, Guang Wudi 光武帝, was enthroned at Luo which then became an important capital and economic centre.[4] Its name did not change to Luoyang until the Three Kingdom period (AD 220–280) during which many internal power struggles took place. Wei Wendi 魏文帝 shifted his capital to Luoyang and built his palace and political centre there.[5]

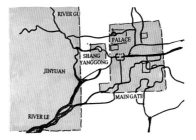

The Three Kingdoms ended in AD 280 by the Jin dynasty which itself lasted until AD 316.[6] In AD 311 Luoyang was sacked and the emperor captured. With the downfall of the Western Jin and the sacking of Luoyang, many learned men fled to south China.[7] During the reign of Xiao Wendi 孝文帝 (AD 471–499) in the North Wei era (AD 386–534), Luoyang was the cultural and political centre of ancient China.[8] Architecture flourished and many temples were built. According to the *Luoyang Jialan Ji* 洛阳伽蓝记 more than forty temples were constructed. The largest was the Yong Ningsi 永宁寺 which consisted of a *shanmen*, a pagoda and prayer halls.

The main street, Tong Tuo 铜驼, divided the city into two. In the north was the imperial, government and public administrative centre, while in the south was the recreational and landscaped area. The most important area was centred along the axial line of the city. The landscape of the imperial area of Luoyang during the North Wei era is recorded in the *Luoyang Jialan Ji*.[9]

During the Sui 隋 (AD 581–618) and Tang 唐 (AD 618–907) eras Luoyang's landscape architecture developed further. Although the Sui destroyed Luoyang when it conquered the Wei, emperor Sui Yangdi 隋炀帝 rebuilt it in a grid pattern and connected it with Beijing and Hangzhou by canals. It became an important trading centre. Imperial palaces complete with magnificent landscape gardens were constructed on a larger scale than that of the Wei.[10]

Luoyang's architecture flourished under the rule of the Tang emperor in the seventh century AD when it was the second seat of the government.[11] However, its development was hampered by the Jin conquerers and it has since lost its importance as the political and cultural centre of China.

The most famous temple in Luoyang, the Bai Masi 白马寺 (White Horse Temple),

OPPOSITE: The Longmen caves of Luoyang; ABOVE: Landscape gardens in Luoyang, above, North Wei dynasty; below, Tang dynasty

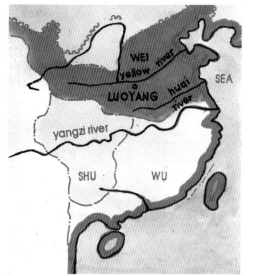

The location of Luoyang during the Three Kingdom era

The unification by the Qin ruler

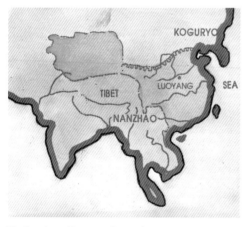

The location of Luoyang during the Tang era

was the first Buddhist temple ever built. It dates back to AD 67 and is so named because it was established by two Indian monks, Matanga and Falan, who brought the sutras to Luoyang riding on white horses. Another story related to the construction of the temple was associated with emperor Han Mingdi 汉明帝. The emperor dreamt of Buddha in the form of a flying golden figure and so he sent his officers to India in search of the sutras. They returned in the company of two Indian monks who brought along the sutras. To house these the Hong Lusi was converted into Bai Masi.[12]

Luoyang is an ancient city with a long historical past, many notable monuments and ancient relics. The huge bronze bell in the Bai Masi, dating back one thousand two hundred and seventy years, is one of the relics of the Sui era. A thirteen-storey masonry pagoda southeast of Bai Masi is believed to be eight hundred years old.

During the Sui and Tang eras the city planning of Luoyang was already very neat and orderly. The imperial palaces were sited west of the northern part of the city.[13] Luoyang was also the commercial and cultural centre of the Tang dynasty. Empress Wu Zetian 武则天 had the cave shrine, Longmen 龙门, developed further and many majestic temples built, including the Feng Xiansi 奉先寺.

The well-known Longmen Caves sited on the sides of the Yi He 伊河 in the south of Luoyang were first discovered in the North Wei era and have survived the test of time through the East and West Wei eras, the North Zhou, the Sui and the North Song periods. In the east and west hills of the Longmen are over two thousand niches housing over one hundred thousand Buddhist images, over three thousand five hundred carved stone steles and forty pagodas. The cave sanctuaries that have become popular are the Gu Yangdong 古阳洞, the Bing Yangdong 槟阳洞, the Lian Fadong 莲花洞 and the Wan Fodong 万佛洞. The Gu Yangdong is situated on the hill in the southern section of the Longmen and was discovered in AD 493. The altar for the Buddha is preceded and flanked by a pair of stone lions carved in dynamic poses. Dating back to the fifth century, the Bing Yangdong actually consists of three caves and is sited on the north hill of the Longmen. The relief carving of the Buddha is almost 8 metres tall, while on the walls beside the Buddha are carved the Tian Wang 天王 (Diamond Kings) who were supposed to suppress evil forces. The central cave of the Bing Yangdong is the most impressive of all. The carvings and artefacts were completed in AD 523. It houses eleven huge statues of the Buddha, one of which is 8.5 metres tall. The Wan Fodong is on the south of the hill of Longmen. Its top, carved like a huge lotus flower, was completed in AD 680. In the cave there are as many as fifteen thousand small icons of the Buddha. A statue of Amitabha was placed on a podium depicting the lotus plant.

The popular temples are the Feng Xiansi 凤先寺, and the Kan Jingsi 看经寺. The Feng Xiansi is sited on the south hillside. Constructed in AD 672 it contains many Tang dynasty carvings that display great skills in the art of sculpture. The statues in the shrine display vivid expressions and fine details. The Kan Jingsi contains numerous Tang dynasty relics.[14] The top portion is made up of coffers depicting lotus plants, symbols of purity.

In the south of Luoyang is the Guanlin 关林, a beautiful wooded area which is believed to house the burial ground of the war hero of the Three Kingdom era, Guan Yu 关羽. A Ming temple named Guan Dimaio 关帝庙 is dedicated to Guan Yu.

During the North Song dynasty (AD 960–923) Luoyang was called Xi Jing 西京, second only to Kaifeng 开封, the capital. It remained a cultural and educational centre. It was renamed Zhong Jing 中京 during the Jin era and continued to be an important cultural city through the Yuan, Ming and Qing dynasties.

Notes

1 See opposite for the map showing the unification by the Qin ruler.

2 Relics providing such evidence have been found. See the article published by the archaeologists on 'Kaogu Xuepao' 考古学报 Vol 2 (Luoyang) 1959.

3 See opposite for sketch map of China during the Warring States.

4 See Cotterell, Arthur, China, *A Concise Cultural History*, John Murray (London) 1988, p113.

5 See Liu Dunzhen 刘敦桢, *Zhongguo Gudai Jianzhu Shi* 中国古代建筑史, Zhongguo Jianzhu Gongye Chuban She 中国建筑工业出版社 (Beijing) 1980, p50.

6 See opposite for the location of Luoyang during the Three Kingdom period and its geographical relationship with the various kingdoms.

7 See Cotterell, Arthur, ibid, p130.

8 Xiao Wendi moved his capital from Pingcheng 平城 to Luoyang and established the capital as a commercial, Buddhist and diplomatic centre. Over one thousand Buddhist temples were built.

9 Refer to the map of Luoyang during the North Wei on p107. Also see Yang Xuanzhi, *Luoyang Jialan Ji* (China) North Wei period. Yang described the imperial garden, Hua Linyuan 华林园, as being sited on the shore of a huge lake. On the lake was a platform on which the emperor Gao Zu 高祖 built the palace Qing Liangdian 清凉殿. In the south was the Xi Youyuan.

10 See Sui Shu 隋书, *Dili Zhi* 地理志, Sui dynasty. It was recorded that Xi Yuan, west of Luoyang, was one of the largest imperial gardens covering an area of 200 square *li* (miles). The commercial network and the Silk Road to other parts of China also started from Luoyang.

11 See opposite for the map of China during the Tang dynasty.

12 See section on Bai Masi on p110-113.

13 See 'Kaogu' 考古 Vol 3, 1961 published by the archaeologists of Luoyang, Zhongguo Kexue Yuan Kaogu Yanjiu Suo 中国科学院考古研究所.

14 Well-known poets such as Li Bai 李白, Du Pu 杜莆 and Bai Juyi 白居易 had left their poetic creations on the cave walls.

白馬寺 洛陽
Baimasi dated 67AD
Sketch by Evelyn Lip 19/9/94

Bai Masi

The first major Buddhist temple built in Henan and still in existence is the Bai Masi 白马寺. It is situated in the western part of Luoyang and was built in AD 67 on the site of the Hong Lusi 鸿胪寺 which was once used as a reception hall for residing foreign diplomats.[1] The group of buildings was rebuilt and became a Buddhist temple.[2] Although the temple is dated Han, many renovations have taken place and some parts were reconstructed during the Ming dynasty.[3]

The entrance gateway is in three sections; the main central part is higher than the side entrance arches and is covered by a half-hipped/half-gabled roof. The roofs of the side arches butt the sides of the main entrance block. The masonry gateway is painted red. The signboard bears the name of Bai Masi in white.[4] Outside the arched entrances is a pair of stone horses dating back to the Qing period.

The temple complex, surrounded by a yellow masonry wall, comprises a series of halls forming four internal courtyards. The first prayer hall is the Yuan dynasty Tian Wangdian 天王殿 (the Hall of the Heavenly Kings). In this hall icons of the Maitreya Buddha (the Heavenly Kings) and Wei Tuo are placed.[5]

The second hall is the main prayer hall and is called Da Fodian 大佛殿 (the Big Buddha Hall).[6] In it is a gilded statue of Buddha Sakyamuni flanked by Wen Shu 文殊 and Pu Xian 普贤.[7]

The third prayer hall, the Da Xiong Baodian 大雄宝殿 (the Great Heroes Hall) is for the worship of the main deities, the Buddhas and the Eighteen Luohans (Arhats) The statues of the Luohans date back to the Ming dynasty. On the walls are painted five hundred images of the Buddha.

Beyond the Da Xiong Baodian is a complex which consists of the tallest structure, the Pi Luge 毗卢寺. It was formerly used by the Han emperor as a library for keeping the sutras and for viewing the surroundings. In this hall statues of the Buddha are kept. The most impressive architecturally is the main prayer hall, the Jie Yingdian 接英殿 (Reception Hall), built by the Ming emperor, Ming Di. It is covered by a two-tiered half-hipped/half-gabled roof.

On the east of the temple complex is the Qi Yunta 齐云塔, a thirteen-storey masonry pagoda, measuring 7.8 by 7.8 metres with a height of 35 metres. A south-facing door is opened on every two floors. This pagoda was built in AD 1175. Another pagoda, named Wen Fengta 文峰塔 situated at the southeast of Luoyang, is a nine-storey pagoda, 28.5 metres high and built with bricks. The highest level of the pagoda is punctuated by four doors. Originally the structure was dated Song era but as it was destroyed in the Ming dynasty its present form is dated during the Qing era.

Northeast of Luoyang is situated the tomb of the Han dynasty Guang Wudi 光武帝. Many ancient tomb remains are found on the Mangshan, north of Luoyang. In the south part of Luoyang over the Luo He 洛河 is the well-known Tian Jinqiao 天津桥, originally known as Luo Yangqiao 洛阳桥. On this bridge is a pavilion covered by a pyramidal roof. It was built in AD 605.

To the north is an interesting temple named Lu Zumiao 吕祖庙, built by emperor

Qian Long. It is dedicated to one of the Eight Immortals, Lu Dong Bin 吕洞宾. The site is enhanced by the Mangshan at its rear and the Chan Shui 缠水 river.

On the west side of Luoyang is Zhou Gongmiao 周公庙, a temple dated Sui dynasty, which was built by the Sui warrior, Wang Shi Chong 王世充.[8]

At the south gate of Luoyang is an interesting brick building designed using the courtyard concept. It was used by the Nationalists as anti-Japanese headquarters during the Japanese war. It is now a museum for the display of war weapons and medals won by the Nationalists who fought against the Japanese.

Notes

1 In AD 65 the emperor Han Mingdi 明帝 of the East Han dynasty sent envoys to India to aquire the sutras. The two envoys returned with two Indian monks, Falan 法兰 and Matanga, who became the principal abbots of Bai Masi. When the monks arrived they were riding white horses.

2 The design and planning of a temple was similar in principle to a major residence or palace. Emperor Yong Zheng's residence was converted into a temple when he ascended the throne. See Qi Ying Tao 祁英涛, *Zhongguo Gujian Zhushi Qide Jianding* 中国古建筑时期得键定. Wenwu 文物 (Beijing) 1965, Vol 4, pp17-18.

3 The stone stele relates the dates of construction and renovations of the temple. It was also renovated during the Song, Yuan and Qing eras.

4 This was dated AD 1546.

5 Wei Tuo is the protector of the Buddhist faith. He is usually portrayed standing upright, wearing an ancient suit of armour and a sword which may be used to strike those who damage the Buddhist relics.

6 This is the main prayer hall and houses the Sakyamuni Buddha who is regarded as the spiritual leader of the Buddhists. Sakyamuni was an Indian prince born in the sixth century near Nepal. He gave up his princely life to seek the truth and peace and he attained enlightenment.

7 Refer to the section on Buddhism on p16. Wen Shu and Pu Xian were the disciples of the Buddha.

8 See *Zizhi Tongjian* 资治通鉴. Zhou Gong 周公 was the fourth son of Zhou Wen Wang 周文王. He helped his brother, Wu Wang 武王, conquer the tyrant Shang emperor.

Yin and *yang* stone lions

The bell tower of the Bai Masi

Shao Linsi

Shao Linsi was named after its location, situated in the forest (lin 林) of the Wuyu 五乳 (five peaks) foothills of the Shao Shishan 少室山 in the Deng Fengxian 登封县 of Henan 河南. Its temple complex, consisting of five thousand halls, spreads over a huge site of 1,400 acres and its resident monks number over one thousand.[1] There are various types of structure in the Shao Linsi including gateways, pagodas, pavilions, temples and numerous carved stone panels. The Xiao Qi river flows past the main entrance which is flanked by stone lions. A stone bridge spans over the river. The entrance hall, shanmen 山门, leads to the open gallery of carved stone panels, carved and executed with great skill. The first major hall is the Tian Wangdian. The site beyond the Tian Wangdian and the open courtyard originally housed the Daxiong Baodian 大雄宝殿 and the Fatang 法堂. The Fazhang 法丈 hall and monks' quarters form a si heyuan 四合院 (buildings grouped around a courtyard). The Li Xueting 立雪亭, the Di Cangdian 地藏殿, the Qian Fodian 千佛殿, which are dated Ming dynasty, are to the rear of the complex.[2] The Qian Fodian is one of the main prayer halls and it was built in AD 1588. On its walls are painted five hundred arhats. Its floor is marked by forty-eight foot prints, formed by the feet of the monks who practised martial arts in the hall. To the east is situated the Bai Yidian 白衣殿, famous for the wall murals of monks practising Shaolin martial arts. The west side of the complex houses the Gan Lutai, a Buddhist temple complex that was built by Fotuo Dashi and dates back to the fifth century AD.

During the reign of Xiao Wendi 孝文帝 (AD 471–500) of the North Wei era, Luoyang was made the capital city and under imperial patronage the Buddhist religion flourished. Hundreds of temples were built and Shao Linsi was one of the most outstanding. Its first pioneer abbot was Fotuo Dashi 佛陀大师, an Indian monk who brought Indian sutras, which were then translated into Chinese. The second abbot was Da Mo 大摩 who was said to be the twenty-ninth generation disciple of Buddha Sakyamuni. He taught his disciples how to read the sutras and to meditate.[3] His assistant abbot was Hui Ke 慧可. Shao Linsi underwent significant periods of historical development and turmoil. Although it enjoyed a period of triumph with the support of the North Wei emperors, by the sixth century AD in the North Zhou (AD 557–581) era it suffered a major decline when the imperial household turned to Taoism which was promoted nationwide. However, the last of the North Zhou emperors, Jing Di 景帝, reintroduced Buddhism and re-established the Shao Linsi as the Zhi Husi 陟岵寺 (temple on the hill with many plants).

By the Sui dynasty (AD 581–618) the emperor promoted Buddhism further and Zhi Husi reverted back to its original name, Shao Linsi. The Tang dynasty (AD 618–907) was the most important era in the history of China in terms of architectural, cultural and religious development. Shao Linsi was rebuilt and extended; and it continued to be one of the major temples in China until the Yuan dynasty (AD 1206–1368) when it burnt down. Although it was later reconstructed most of the ancient halls were ruined.

Sketch location of Shao Linsi

Shao Linsi is made up of several parts: the Chang Zhuyuan 长住院, the group of pagodas, the platform of dews, the Er Zuan 二祖庵, the Chu Zuan 初祖庵 and the Da Modong 达摩洞. In the Chang Zhuyuan are countless bas-reliefs of poetic writings by famous calligraphers and Buddhist figures such as the Goddess of Mercy and the Buddha.[4] The carving techniques, typical of Shaolin style, and introduced by Han and Wei dynasty artisans, were executed with great vigour.[5]

The Chang Zhuan is a nunnery dedicated to the founder of the Chen sect. It consists of a large worship hall dating back to the North Song era (tenth century AD). The main pillars of the hall are octagonal in section and they are skilfully carved with fascinating Buddhist figures. The twelve peripheral columns are furthermore also carved with dancing figures.

At the west of the temple complex is the Talin 塔林 which in effect is the burial place of the monks. There are as many as two hundred and fifty pagodas in the Talin. Built during different eras they were designed in various styles.

In the northwest of the temple complex are the Chu Zhuan and the Da Modong; both were built to commemorate Da Mo, the founder.

Notes

1 See Su Siyi 苏思义 et al, *Shao Linsi Shike Yishu Xuan* 少林寺石刻义术选, Wenwu Chuban She 文物出版社 (Beijing) 1985, p1. See sketch of the Shao Linsi opposite.

2 Li Xueting, dated Qing dynasty, survived the fire in 1928. It obtained its name because Da Mo's disciple, Hui Ke 慧可, convinced him that he was determined to become a monk by cutting off his left arm and standing at the front door for hours until Da Mo accepted him as his disciple.

3 It was said that Da Mo was an expert in martial arts and he trained the monks in practising the Shao Linquan 少林拳.

4 Well-known poets and calligraphers included Pei Cui 裴崔 of the Tang dynasty, Mi Fu 米芾 of the Song dynasty, Meng Fu of the Yuan dynasty and Dong Qichang 董其昌 of the Ming dynasty.

5 Some carved panels showed the practice of Syncretism (a practice combining Buddhism, Taoism and Confucianism). One carved panel dated during the Jin dynasty portrayed the images of the Buddha, Lao Zi and Confucius. Another dated during the Ming dynasty showed a number of figures representing various religious beliefs.

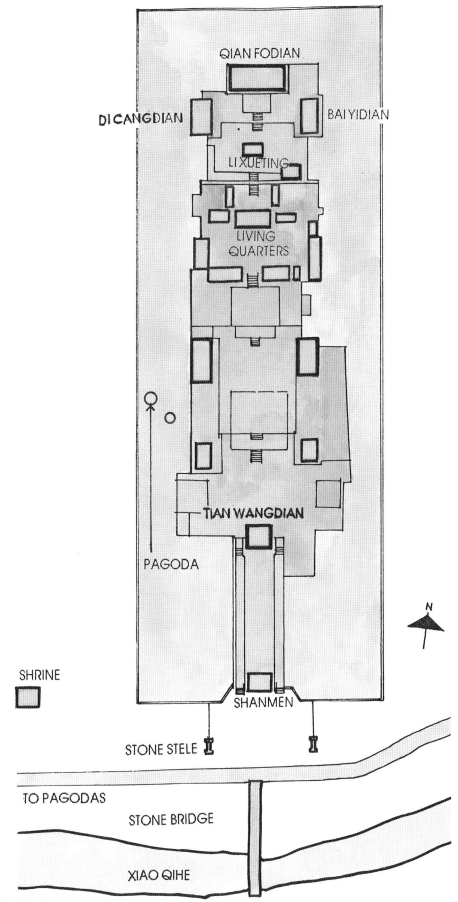

QIAN FODIAN

DI CANGDIAN

BAI YIDIAN

LI XUETING

LIVING QUARTERS

PAGODA

TIAN WANGDIAN

SHRINE

SHANMEN

N

STONE STELE

TO PAGODAS

STONE BRIDGE

XIAO QIHE

Block plan of the Shao Linsi

Other Historical Temples and Structures in Luoyang

This section gives brief descriptions of some of the religious buildings in Luoyang. The architectural planning and detail of the buildings are omitted as they are typical and are modelled upon the traditional Chinese style of architecture.

Yong Ningsi 永宁寺

East of Bai Masi are the remains of one of Luoyang's historical buildings, the Yong Ningsi, which was built during the reign of Zheng Guang 正光 (AD 520–525). At that time the Buddhist faith was strongly supported by the ruling class and there were as many as thirty thousand Buddhist temples in China. In the city of Luoyang alone there were over one thousand temples and among them the Yong Ningsi was the largest.[1] The temple was patronised by empress dowager Hu 胡太后.[2]

The entrance to the temple complex was through four gateways. The south gate was an imposing three-tier structure. The prayer hall of Yong Ningsi housed a huge gilded statue of the Buddha approximately 2 metres high. This statue was flanked by another ten gilded statues. Beyond the prayer hall were hundreds of smaller but ornately finished buildings for the residence of the monks. South of the prayer hall was a nine-tier timber pagoda approximately 90 metres tall. Even though these monumental structures have been ruined, the foundations are still in existence.

Shang Qinggong 上清宫

Situated on the hills of Cui Yunfeng 翠云峰 (a part of the Mangshan 邙山) and enclosed by high walls, the Shang Qinggong was built during the reign of Tang Gaozong 唐高宗 in AD 666. It was originally a Taoist temple complex with four courtyards and a series of prayer halls.

The temple was popular because the caves around it, especially the Cui Yundong, were summer resorts for people who stayed near and far. Within the caves there were prayer halls such as the Yu Huangge.

The temple was destroyed by the Jin invaders but was rebuilt in AD 1545.[3] Some of the structural members were replaced by metal components and its roofs were upgraded to glazed tiled roofs.

The single-storey Yu Huangge built with fair-faced brick, appears modest in terms of architectural treatment and finishing. Its windows are rectangular openings with vertical bars. Its central bay consists of four panels of timber door with square latticework.

Zhou Gongmiao 周公庙

To the west of the city of Luoyang is situated the Sui dated Zhou Gongmiao. The temple was built by Wang Shichong 王世充, a warrior of the Sui dynasty (AD 581–618). When Wang was attacking an enemy camp he had it made known to his soldiers that Zhou Gong 周公, a West Zhou politician and a brother of Zhou Wuwang 周武王, had appeared in the dreams of one of the warriors and informed him that he would assist Wang in his endeavours.[4] Wang therefore built the temple in honour of Zhou Gong to give confidence to his soldiers that he would be the victor.[5] The temple is still patronised and, as it stands today, consists of two prayer halls and a number of residential quarters. The main prayer hall is covered by a half-hipped/half-gabled roof. The walls of the hall are of masonry.

Longmen 龙门

South of Luoyang are the famous caves of the Longmen which are noted for their auspicious *feng shui* and countless Buddhist sculptures. To its east are the hills of Xiang Shan 香山 and its west the hills of Long Menshan 龙门山. In between the hills is the Yi Shui 伊水 river.

The Longmen consists of two thousand one hundred caves, one hundred thousand statues of Buddhist figures, two thousand eight hundred and seventy engraved stone steles and forty pagodas. These Buddhist relics are the efforts of artisans over a long historical period (from the North Wei in the fourth century AD to the tenth century AD in the North Song dynasty).

In the caves are some famous temples namely the Bing Yangdong 槟阳洞 and the Feng Xiansi 奉先寺; the former houses carved Buddhist images and calligraphic writings dating back to the fifth century AD while the latter houses large Buddhist figures carved out of the caves.[6]

Summary

Throughout the history of China there was never any serious tension between sacred and secular domains. Very often secular philosophical views and religious beliefs seemed to merge. The imperial thrones were closely associated with religious rituals and it was the duty of the rulers of the thrones to perform religious ceremonies. As the emperors were direct descendants from the heavens they were placed in the unique position of being sons of the heavens and patrons of religious centres. Many temples were built with great grandeur in terms of scale and finishing.

Notes

1 He Guanbao 贺官保, *Luoyang Wenwu yu Guji* 洛阳文物与古迹, Wenwu Chuban She 文物出版社 (China) nd p37.

2 See *Luoyang Jialan Ji*, op cit.

3 Shang Qinggong is still in existence even though some of its structures have perished.

4 Zhou Gong assisted his brother in bringing to an end the reign of the tyrant Shang emperor. When his brother Wu Wang died, he became the most powerful protector and administrator of the throne of his nephew.

5 See Si Maguang 司马光, *Zizhi Tongjian* 资治通鉴, Song dynasty, republished by Guji Chuban She 古迹出版社 in 1956.

6 See illustration on p106.

Epilogue

The preceding chapters have attempted to weave the brief historical and religious background of China and many aspects of Chinese architecture and landscape, together with detailed descriptions of the planning, architecture and metaphysical conditions of the imperial palaces of the Ming and Qing eras. The lack of conflict between the various religious denominations and the lack of tension between the secular and the sacred enhance the imperial ruler's position as the political and religious head of his people.

The general architectural characteristics of traditional buildings in China depict themes and concepts characteristic of traditional China. The Chinese concept of planning and designing the environment, the system of construction and detailing of decorative motifs clearly reflect the extent to which religious, political and metaphysical influences were exerted upon them. The planning is based on Confucian precepts, the landscaping on Taoist ideas and the overall design of traditional buildings is closely related to imperial and feudalistic systems.

The imperial ruler, at the apex of the earthly hierarchy, was also the son of the heavens and the mediator between man and heaven. Therefore, he had to be seen as such, balanced and wise, and residing in palaces designed with symmetry and in line with the four directions of the heavens. It was imperative that he faced south during an audience with his subjects so that he would meet the divine gaze of the heavens. His palaces lay along the heavenly meridian, sited on auspicious ground in perfect harmony with all the surrounding metaphysical features, planned with reference to geomantic precepts and furnished as well as finished with the most auspicious symbols and jewels. These palatial structures were of the grandest scale and the most imposing spatial and architectural treatments. Building elements had to be balanced in terms of *yin* and *yang* which were constantly interacting to produce energy. The natural harmony of the palaces and the capital cities was not to be disturbed at any cost, because the success or failure of the ruler could be affected by adverse or unfavourable environments or conditions. If the ruler failed to bring prosperity, happiness and peace to his people it would be seen as a sign or response from the heavens that he was no longer fit to rule. Thus, the Forbidden City and the Gugong were built with powerful symbols, in a protected and dignified environment to consolidate his political position.

The imperial ruler was also seen as the arbiter of justice; as such, he had to pray to his ancestors and his gods for blessings, prosperity and good harvests in the supreme form of worship at the most ornate and grandest religious buildings, including the Temple of Heavens and the Altar of Heaven.

The need to create the best *feng shui* sites complete with the ideal cosmological influence required the development of landscape design to complement the architecture of palatial buildings. Artificial hills, man-made lakes and all forms of symbols and sculptures were created for the enhancement of the built environment of summer and retirement palaces. The balance of *yin* and *yang* elements and the favourable workings of the Five Elements were applied to landscape design as much as to building design. Harmony between man and the cosmos had to be achieved through harmony in nature. The Yi Heyuan and the Bishu Shanzhuang were, indeed, models of powerful landscaped summer palaces that enhanced the majesty of the imperial rulers.

In the past, Chinese temples were not just religious buildings but also tourist attractions. They were used by imperial rulers to reinforce their position in society as spiritual leaders linking man and heaven. Like the imperial palaces they were sited on auspicious ground with desirable physical and natural features to enhance their external environment. Beijing's Temple of Heaven, Altar of Heaven and Yong Hegong were and, still are, some of the most notable religious buildings ever constructed. The external form and the internal spatial effect are significantly ornate and magnificent. The symbols and decorative motifs applied on the structural and decorative elements truly reflect the supreme political and economic power their patrons possessed.

Indeed, the historical buildings, still existing in the cities of Beijing and Luoyang, bear testimony to the glorious eras of the Ming and Qing dynasties and reflect the supreme authority of the imperial rulers. The imperial palaces were constructed not just for dwelling or administrating the affairs of a nation but also for reinforcing and confirming the supernatural as well as the earthly authority of the emperors. The landscaped gardens of imperial summer retreats and palaces were built with artificial lakes and man-made hills to depict the most desirable built environment that would invoke the harmony of nature and rejuvenate the energy of man. These gardens provide a conducive and harmonious setting for powerful and magnificent buildings worthy of the sons of the heavens.

Bibliography

Chinese References

Ban Gu 班固, *Han Shu* 汉书 (China) Han dynasty.

Ceng Zinan 曾子南, *Sanyuan Dili Tuwen Qianjie* 三元地理图文浅解 (Taipei) 1965.

Chen Lifu 陈立夫, *Kongzi Xueshu* 孔子学书 (Taiwan) 1960.

Chen Meng Lei 陈梦雷 and Qing Jiangting 清蒋廷, *Gujin Tushu Jicheng* 古金图书集成 (China) Qing dynasty.

Ji Cheng 计成, *Yuan Yi* 园治 (China) Ming dynasty.

Fang Xuanling 房玄龄, *Jin Shu* 晋书 (China) Tang dynasty.

Feng Shui Guaitan 风水怪谈 (Hong Kong) 1963.

Ge Hong 葛洪, *Xijing Zaji* 西京杂记 (China) Jin dynasty.

Gongcheng Zuofa 工程作法 (China) 1732.

Jia Junying 贾俊英 and Zheng Lianzhang 郑连章, *Zi Jincheng Gongdian Wuding Shiyang* 紫禁城宫殿屋顶式样 (China) 1980.

Jiang Pingjie 蒋平楷, *Dili Zhengshu* 地理正疏 (Taiwan) 1980.

Li Jie 李诫, *Yingzao Fashi* 营造法式, Vol 4 (China) 1097.

Li Jianren 李健人, *Luoyang Gujin Tan* 洛阳古金谈, Shixue Yanjiu She 史学研究社 (China) 1936.

Liang Sicheng 梁思成, *Qing Gugong Wen* 清古宫文, *Yuange Shice Tushuo* 渊阁实测图说, Zhongguo Yingzuo Xueshe 中国营造学社 (China).

Liu Dunzhen 刘敦桢, *Zhongguo Gudai Jianzhu Shi* 中国古代建筑史, Zhongguo Jianzhu Gongye Chuban She 中国建筑工业出版社 (China) 1984.

Liu Qijun 刘奇俊, *Zhongguo Gujian Zhu* 中国古建筑, Yishu Jia Chuban She 艺术家出版社 (Taibei) 1987.

Liu Ruoyu 刘若愚, *Ming Gongshi* 明宫史 (China) Ming dynasty.

Lu Dalin 吕大临, *Kaogu Tu* 考古图 (China) 1092.

Meng Yuanlao 孟元老, *Dongjing Menghua Lu* 东京梦华录, Song dynasty.

Nan Haiguan 南海关, *Kanyu Xueyuan Li* 堪舆学原理 (Hong Kong) 1971.

Pan Guxi 潘谷西, *Zhongguo Jianzhu* 中国建筑, Zhongguo Jianzhu Gongye Chuban She 中国建筑工业出版社 (Beijing) 1982.

Pan Guxi 潘谷西, *Woguo Gudai Yuanlin Fazhan Gaiguan* 我国古代 园林 发展概观, Shanghai keji Chuban She 上海科技出版社 (Shanghai) 1980.

Qinghua Daxue Jianzhu Xibian 清华大学建筑系编, *Zhongguo Gudai Jianzhu* 中国古代建筑, Qinghua Daxue Chuban She (Beijing) 1985.

Qinghua Daxue Jianzhu Xi 清华大学建筑系, *Jianzhu Shi Lunwen Ji* 建筑史论文集, Qinghua Daxue Chuban She (Beijing) 1983.

Ren Jiyu 任继愈 (ed), *Zhongguo Wen Hua Shi Zhishi Cong Shu* 中国文化史知识丛书, *Zhongguo Gu Dai Jian Zhu*, Zhong Gong Zhong Yang Dang Xiao Chu Ban She 中国中央党校出版社, 1991.

Ruan Yuandeng 阮元等, *Guangdong Tongzhi* 广东通志 (Taiwan) Qing dynasty.

Ru Jinhua 茹竞华, *Cining Huayuan* 慈宁花园, Gugong Bowu Yuankan 故宫博物院刊, (Beijing) 1981.

Sima Qian 司马迁, *Shiji* 史记 (China) Han dynasty.

Tiangong Kaiwu 天工开物 (China) 1637.

Tianjin Daxue Jianzhu Gongcheng Xi 天津大学建筑工程系, *Qingdai Neiting Gongyuan* 清代内廷宫苑 Tianjin Daxue Chuban She 天津大学出版社 (Tianjin) 1986.

Tianjin Daxue Jianzhu Xi 天津大学建筑系, *Chengde Gu Jianzhu* 承德古建筑, Chengde Wenwu Ju 承德文物局 (China) 1982.

Wang Yunwu 王云五, *Zhongguo Jianzhu Shi* 中国建筑史 (Shanghai) 1926.

Xie Yixian 谢易显, *Yishu Xianyi* 易术显义 (Hong Kong) 1978.

Yu Minzhong 于敏中, *Guochao Gongshi* 国朝宫史, Dongfang Xuehui 东方学会, (China) 1925.

Yu Zhuoyun 于倬云, *Zi Jincheng Gongdian* 紫禁城宫殿, The Commercial Press (Hong Kong) 1982.

Zhou Weiquan 周维权, *Beijing Xibei Jiaode Yuanlin* 北京西北郊的园林, Qinghua Daxue Chuban She (Beijing) 1979.

English References

Arlington, L C and Lewisohn, W, *In Search of Old Peking*, The French Bookstore 1935.

Ball, Dyer, *Things Chinese*, Scribrier's Sons (New York) 1904.

Bagenal, Philip and Meades, Jonathan, *Great Buildings*, Salamander Books Limited (London) 1980.

Birch, C, *Anthology of Chinese Literature*, Grove Press (London) 1965.

Bring, Mitchell, and Josse, W, *Japanese Garden Design and Meaning*, (New York) 1981.

Burkhardt, V R, *Chinese Creeds and Customs*, South China Morning Post Ltd (Hong Kong) 1982.

Chang, K C, *Art, Myth and Ritual, The Path to Political Authority in Ancient China*, Harvard University Press (London) 1983.

Creel, H G, *The Birth of China: A survey of the Formative Period of Chinese Civilization*, Jonathan Cape (London) 1936.

Dawson, R, (ed), *The Legacy of China*, Oxford University Press (Oxford) 1964.

De Bary, W T, *Buddhism and The Chinese Tradition*, East Asian Institute, School of International Affairs, Columbia University Press (New York) 1965.

De Bary, W T, Chan, W T, and Watson, B, *Sources of Chinese Tradition*, Columbia University Press (New York) 1960.

Dore, Henry, *Research into Chinese Superstitions*, Tusewei Printing Press, (Shanghai) 1928.

Eitel, E J, *Feng Shui or the Rudiments of Natural Science in China*, Lane Crawford (Hong Kong) 1973.

Feng Yulan, *A Short History of Chinese Philosophy*, The Free Press (London) 1966.

Fletcher, Banister, *A History of Architecture on the Comparative Method*, B T Batsford (London) 1958.

Ho, P T, *The Cradle of the East*, The University of Chicago Press (Chicago) 1975.

Johnston, R F, *Buddhist China*, John Murray (London) 1913.

—, *Twilight in the Forbidden City*, Gollancz (London) 1934.

Keigthley, D N, (ed), *The Origins of Chinese Civilization*, University of California Press (London) 1983.

Keswick, M, *The Chinese Garden, History, Art and Architecture*, Academy Editions (London) 1978.

Legge, James, *Lichi, the Book of Rites*, University Books (New York) 1967.

Loewe, Michael, *Imperial China: the Historical Background to the Modern Age*, Allen & Unwin (London) 1966.

Lindqvist, C, *China, Empire of Living Symbols*, Addison-Wesley (New York) 1989.

Lip, Evelyn, *Chinese Geomancy*, Times Books International (Singapore) 1979.

—, 'Feng Shui, Chinese Colours and Symbolism', *Singapore Institute of Architects Journal* (Singapore) July, 1978.

—, 'Geomancy and Building', *Development and Construction* (Singapore) 1977.

—, *Chinese Temples and Deities*, Times Books International (Singapore) 1981.

—, *Fun With Chinese Horoscopes*, Graham Brash (Singapore) 1981.

—, *Chinese Temple Architecture in Singapore*, Singapore University Press (Singapore) 1983.

—, *Chinese Beliefs and Superstitions*, Graham Brash (Singapore) 1985.

—, *Chinese Proverbs and Sayings*, Graham Brash (Singapore) 1985.

—, *Chinese Customs and Festivals*, Macmillan Education (London) 1985.

—, *Feng Shui for the Home*, Times Books International (Singapore) 1986.

—, *Feng Shui for Business*, Times Books International, reprinted by Times Editions (Singapore) 1987.

—, *Choosing Auspicious Chinese Names*, Times Books International (Singapore) 1988.

—, *Notes on Things Chinese*, Graham Brash (Singapore) 1988.

—, *Out of China, Culture and Traditions*, Addison-Wesley (Singapore) 1993.

—, *The Design and Feng Shui of Logos, Trademarks and Signboards*, Simon & Schuster (Asia) Pte Ltd (Singapore) 1994.

Moller, J, *Chinese Buddhist Monasteries*, Oxford University Press (Oxford) 1937.

Munsterberg, H, *A Short History of Chinese Art*, Peter Owen, (London) 1954.

Needham, Joseph, *Science and Civilization in China*, Cambridge University Press (Cambridge) 1982.

Rawson J, *Ancient China, Art and Archaeology*, British Museum (London) 1980.

Sickman, L, and Soper, A, *The Art and Architecture of China*, Reinhold Publishing Corporation (London) 1968.

Siren, O, *The Chinese on the Art of Painting*, Schocken Books (New York) 1963.

—, *Gardens of China*, Ronald Press Co (New York) 1949.

Su, G D, *Chinese Architecture – Past and Contemporary*, Sin Poh Amalgamated (Hong Kong) 1964.

Van Over, Raymond, *I Ching*, New American Library (Chicago) 1971.

Weber, M, *The Religions of China*, Free Press (London) 1964.

Wilhelm, Richard, *The I Ching or Book of Changes* (London) 1951.

Willets, William, *Chinese Art* (London) 1958.

Yap, Y, and Cotterell, A, *Chinese Civilization*, St Martin's Press (New York) 1977.

Zhong, Y H, (ed), *History and Development of Ancient Chinese Architecture*, Chinese Academy of Sciences, Science Press (Beijing) 1986.

Glossary

an	Buddhist nunnery	*guan*	official
babai	Eighth Essence of the Stars related to the Earth Element	*hai*	harm
		heng	rafter, also; *shang jinheng, zhong jinheng, xia jinheng*
banwa	roof tile		
baoding	decorative element at the termination point of a roof	*houyan qiang*	rear facade wall
		hua limu	high quality hardwood
baozhu	pearl-like	*huangcheng*	royal city
baozuo	imperial seat	*jiaoshou*	roof tile decoration
ben	origin	*jie*	robbed
bing	sickness	*jinhu*	golden lake
cai	prosperity; also unit of measurement equal to 15 *fen*	*jinshan*	gold hill
		jinzhuan	gold paving slabs
chang	hidden	*jiuzi*	Ninth Essence of the Stars related to the Fire Element
changlang	long corridor		
Chengu	clear lake	*Juixing*	system of *feng shui* based on the stars
cheng jianzhuan	finely textured brick used for paving	*kanyu*	Chinese art of placement, see also *feng shui*
chengzhuan	brick used for podiums	*kou*	mouth
chi	fish dragon	*lang*	corridor
chuanting	boat with shelter	*langqiang*	end piece of end wall
chuishou	animal roof tile ornament	*li*	separation; also unit of measure (mile)
ci	temple, usually dedicated to ancestor worship	*liang*	beam; also *qi jialiang, san jialiang* and *wu jialiang*
daode	virtue	*ligong*	resort palace
dian	hall	*lin*	forest
difu	stone mount with grooves to receive balustrades	*liqi*	energy according to the geography of land creating water
		lishui	
dougong	structural timber brackets	*liubi*	Sixth Essence of the Stars related to the Gold Element
dushu	study		
erhei	Second Essence of the Stars related to the Earth Element	*lou*	buildings
		louge	buildings and outhouses
fang	stone boat	*lu*	exposed; also form of roof
fangzhuan	type of brick	*luopan*	geomantic compass
fen	unit of measurement, approximately equal to 1cm	*mending*	metal bosses on doors originally used to hide nail marks
feng shui	harmony and balance in nature with reference to man-made elements, considering aspects of climatology, geophysics, cultural and social issues, metaphysical and cosmological influences	*menhuan*	metal mounts
		menhai	doors of the sea, water vessels
		miao	temple, usually for Syncretist followers
		ming	fate
		nanmu	high quality hardwood
feilong	dancing dragons	*neichao*	residential section of imperial palaces
ge	outhouses and pavilions	*nian*	year
geduan qiang	internal partition wall	*pailou*	entrance gate
gong	temple, usually Taoist in denomination	*pingfeng*	decorative screen

qi	life's energy; also unit of measurement equal to six *fen*	*tang*	halls
qian	northwest direction	*tian*	paddy fields
qichi	Seventh Essence of the Stars related to the Gold Element	*tianhua*	false ceiling
		tianzi	sons of the heavens
qiao	bridge	*tiao*	unit of measurement equal to or more than 30 *fen*
quiang	garden wall		
quzhe jiuzhi	contrast of curved and straight lines	*ting*	pavilion
ren	man; also quality of benevolence	*tongwa*	roof tile
sanbi	Third Essence of the Stars related to the Wood Element	*waichao*	public administration section of imperial palaces
san heyuan	courtyard concept based on symmetry, axial planning and three building blocks	*wen*	mythical creatures used as roof decorations
		wenshou	roof tile ornament
shan	hill	*wuwang*	Fifth Essence of the Stars related to the Earth Element
shang	up		
shangyuan	one of the three cycles of change, a period of sixty years	*xianren*	a fairy roof decoration used to terminate corner of rib
shanmen	entrance gate	*xiayuan*	one of the three cycles of change, a period of sixty years
shanqiang	central end gable wall		
shaqi	excessively vibrant energy	*yang*	metaphysical quality which is solid, positive, material
she	void		
shi	solid	*yanqian youjing*	view or vista to the front
shizhiji	roof form	*yi*	righteousness; also the energy in the inter-action between negative and positive qualities in nature
shouwen	symbol on roof ridge		
shui	water		
shumi deyi	contrast of open and closed	*yibai*	First Essence of the Stars related to the Water Element
si	temple, usually for Buddhist worship		
si heyuan	courtyard concept based on symmetry, axial planning, north/south orientation and wall enclosures formed with four building blocks	*yin*	metaphysical quality which is fluid, negative, spiritual
		Yinhu	silver lake
siku quanshu	collection of the Four Treasures of Knowledge	*yinqi*	negative energy
		yong	bravery
silu	Fourth Essence of the Stars related to the Wood Element	*yun*	periods of luck
		zaojing	caisson
siqi	harmful energy	*zhai*	meditation areas for vegetarians
suozhu	basic column; also five commonly used Qing columns are *chongyan jinzhu, jinzhu, tongzhu, yanzhu* and *zhongzhu*	*zhe*	a tree
		zhi	intelligence
		zhizhu	column, see *suozhu*
stupa	a domed edifice housing Buddhist relics	*zhiwu peizhi*	placing elements in the appropriate positions
sun	southeast direction	*zhongyuan*	middle of the three cycles of change, a period of sixty years
ta	pagoda		
tai	raised platforms	*zhu*	column
		zhu shan	making hills

Index

*Page references in italics refer to
illustrations.*